# Making Sense of Life and Death

## by Larry Walston

*Larry Walston*

Jude 24-25

# TABLE OF CONTENTS

Prologue......................................................................................vii

Part I: Life...................................................................................11
    Chapter 1:  Origin............................................................13
    Chapter 2:  Shape.............................................................21
    Chapter 3:  Direction........................................................28
    Chapter 4:  Purpose..........................................................36
    Chapter 5:  Meaning..........................................................43
    Chapter 6:  Intention........................................................51
    Chapter 7:  Distraction......................................................58
    Chapter 8:  Action............................................................65
    Chapter 9:  Commitment......................................................73
    Chapter 10: Time...............................................................81
    Chapter 11: Perseverance ................................................88
    Chapter 12: Goal...............................................................96

Part II: Death............................................................................105
    Chapter 13: Inevitability.................................................107
    Chapter 14: Timekeeper ................................................114
    Chapter 15: Aversion......................................................155
    Chapter 16: Postponement.............................................129
    Chapter 17: Hope............................................................136
    Chapter 18: Jerry's story................................................144
    Chapter 19: Jared's story .............................................156

Part III: Life after Life and Death ........................................................ 169
    Chapter 20:  Choices ........................................................ 171
    Chapter 21:  Judgment ................................................... 178
    Chapter 22:  Destination ............................................... 186
    Chapter 23:  Duration ................................................... 193

Epilogue ........................................................................................ 201

# PROLOGUE

"Why am I still here? What do I possibly have to offer?" These were Tony's exact words. Even though it was a year ago, those few words are seared into my brain.

Tony asked me those two questions in the midst of a conversation we were having about him just celebrating his 90th birthday. We were sitting comfortably in his small apartment in an assisted living facility, and we had, as always, begun to explore the deeper things of life.

Tony is one of my favorite people, and a man God has put in my life for the dual purpose of teaching me and blessing me. I only wish I was half as encouraging to him as he has been to me.

But this time I was actually able to help him. More on that later.

Tony's most profound effect on my life has to do with my first book, "Serving an Unpopular God". He was one of only a very few people who read my manuscript before the book was published. He was fascinated with it, knowing that because of the many conversations we had already had at that point it was going to stimulate his mind.

It's probably a true statement that without Tony that book would have never been published, and that the next book, "Learning to Love Church", and this book, would have never been written at all.

I knew God wanted me to write that first book, and I leaned on Him hard to get it done. But oddly enough, once it was written, I let it sit. I was relieved that it was done, and for a while, quite a while actually, I didn't care if it was ever published or not. Tony read the manuscript because he is a reader, and because he was very interested in what I had written, knowing pretty well how my mind works.

Every time I saw him after he read it, he asked me when I was going to do something about getting it published. I never had a good answer, of course. I usually mumbled something like "yeah, I really need to get going on that...."

He just wouldn't leave it alone, and in time I realized that Tony was part of God's plan for the book, that he was in my life for a reason, and that part of *his* purpose in life was to push me into doing what God wanted done.

No one was more thrilled than Tony when that first book was published, and he received one of the first copies with my personal note of gratitude written in it.

So I owe Tony a lot, and now, on the auspicious occasion of his 90th birthday, I was being given an opportunity to help him.

Although Tony has a very sharp mind, his body has had issues, so he had to sell his house and move into the assisted living facility which, although very beautiful and comfortable, felt more like "**a** home" rather than "home" to him. He also had to give up his car, his beloved Cadillac, as he was no longer able to drive. His wife Rita had died some years before, and most of his friends were gone, as well. Despite a very loving and attentive family, Tony felt more like a burden than a man with a purpose.

And thus those two questions.

And here I was, a man who in the 12 months previous to those two questions had experienced the devastating deaths of 3 men close to me, and who, through those deaths, had learned a very great deal about the meaning of life.

And I had learned even more about the Giver of life, God Almighty, who had revealed to me in those experiences things that have left me in awe of Him, and in love with Him, forever.

So I knew the answer to Tony's questions, or I should say I knew enough from what I had discovered to tell him how he could find the answer.

"I don't know, Tony. What do you have to offer? Perhaps 90 years of experience in life, or 90 years of wisdom, or 90 years of seeking, or 90 years of learning. In 90 years you have learned much, and there are people in your life who need to know what you have learned. I can't say who they are, but God will direct you to them if you ask Him."

That is what I told him. I knew it to be true. Tony was still here for a purpose, and knowing God as he does, I think he knew it, too.

As is his wise and thoughtful way, Tony said nothing after I said those words to him. He looked straight at me and said nothing, as if to acknowledge that these were not just my words, but the words given to me by God for Tony.

"I'll have to think about that," was all he said.

But Tony did more than think about it, he did something about it. He looked at the people around him differently, as people who needed his help. Like a man on a mission, he began to truly minister to people far younger than he, to teach them things they needed to know, to get them to find the purpose God had for *them*.

Had I not lived through a year of such incredible sorrow, I would not have been able to answer his questions.

I call that a "dose of God's grace".

The three men who died?

My father Jerry, my stepson Jared, and my friend Bill. My father's death I saw coming, but the other two felt like being hit by lightning or run over by a car. And yet I was more ready for them than I knew.

In this book I will tell you more about each of them, for we have much to learn from them. Much more from their life than from their death, but it is their death that causes us to look at their life...and ours.

Ironic, isn't it?

It is my earnest prayer that this book will get you to examine your life, and your inevitable death, to not just make sense of life, but to give it a joyful, unending purpose and deep, profound meaning.

I will do the typing, but I will rely completely on the Holy Spirit to give me the words. I know He will because He has done it for me before.

This book is in three parts. Part I is about life, and will examine every aspect of it, even the parts you don't particularly wish to examine in your own life.

But let's face it, life is meaningless if all we do is trudge through each day and do nothing but exist. I am pretty sure there is something about your life that is as yet undiscovered by you, and I am praying that this book will help you discover it.

Part II is about death, but it is not morbid or sad. Perhaps scary, but I hope not. It is something we all think about it as little as possible, but increasingly more as we grow older. You will find, however, that as you make sense of death you will end up back at...life.

Part III is about life beyond the life and death of this world. It is the most important part of all, because it is forever.

This book has been two years in the preparation. One year of death, one year of incredible life. One year of surviving the storm, one year of calm. Two years of learning that we were created by and are loved by an incredible, awesome, wonderful God who is aware of **everything** that goes on, and who is always in control.

I pray that this book takes you to a place with Him so personal that every day, every moment of your life has meaning, and that death becomes only a doorway that leads to being with Him forever.

Now join me in walking down that road together.

# Part I

# LIFE

# Chapter 1

# ORIGIN

"O Lord, you have searched me and you know me.
You know when I sit and when I rise;
You perceive my thoughts from afar.
You discern my going out and my lying down;
You are familiar with all my ways.
Before a word is on my tongue you know it completely,
O Lord.
For you created my inmost being;
You knit me together in my mother's womb.
I praise you because I am fearfully and wonderfully made;
Your works are wonderful, I know that full well.
My frame was not hidden from You when I was made in the secret place.
When I was woven together in the depths of the earth,
Your eyes saw my unformed body.
All the days ordained for me were written in your book
Before one of them came to be."

Psalm 139:1-4, 13-16

"The God who made the world and everything in it is the Lord of heaven and earth and does not live in temples built by hands. And he is not served by human hands, as if he needed anything, because he himself gives all men life and breath and everything else. From one man he made every nation of men, that they should inhabit the whole earth; and he determined the times set for them and the exact places where they should live. God did this so that men would seek him and perhaps reach out for him and find him, though he is not far from each one of us. For in him we live and move and have our being."

Acts 17:24-28a

Y ou know how it works, don't you? Someone buys an empty lot in your neighborhood, and at some point some heavy equipment is brought in and a huge hole is dug. Then one day a helicopter comes flying in, hovers over the hole, and drops a huge load of wood.

Each piece of wood lands exactly in the right place, and just like that, a perfectly constructed house stands ready for the new owner.

Oh sure, they still have to paint and carpet and all that but....

Wait a minute, you say! That's not the way it works! That house has to be carefully and meticulously built, one piece of wood and one nail at a time. It takes many people and many hours to build this house.

Okay, you got me on that one. So if I want to build my house, I'll just go to the local unemployment office and hire 1,000 people for one day. They can all take a piece of wood or two, and in no time at all the house will be built and ready for me to move in.

No, you say, that will not work either! The house must be built by experienced craftsmen who are following a precise architectural plan. They must know before they start what they are building, and they must follow the plan exactly for it to turn out that way.

I know what you're thinking. You're thinking I'm being ridiculous. No house is ever built by dropping wood from a helicopter willy-nilly, nor is it built by people who have no idea how to do it.

A nice house, a house brand new and beautiful, a house ready to move into, is not an accident. It not only isn't an accident, it *can't* be.

And *you* aren't an accident, either.

You were made exactly the way you are by the purpose and design of God.

And who is God?

He is the One who created everything...*everything.*

He has always been, and always will be.

He has *all* power...power over life, death, nature, nations, sickness, you name it.

He has *all* knowledge...He knows everything, including what is to come.

He is *everywhere*...He is not limited by time or space.

And here's the really cool part: He loves you, and wants what is best for you.

God, when He created each one of us, also gave us an inherent understanding of our Creator, an inner voice, so to speak, so that we know without a doubt not only that He, God our Creator, exists, but that He made us this way on purpose.

You can imagine God's frustration then, when there are people running around saying that we are all accidents, that there was a bang and a pile of cells, and from that willy-nilly mess came what turned out to be...well, *you*! You can really imagine God's frustration when you realize that He created these people, and put in them an understanding of who He is.

I hate to say this, but it is absolutely true. If you really want to make sense of your life, if you want to begin to develop an understanding of why you are here, you have to start with an understanding of where you came from.

And you can *believe* anything you want about where you came from, but it will never change the truth.

You were created by God.

Once you understand this and embrace this, you will discover it to be the most wonderful and yet most frightening truth you have ever faced.

It is wonderful because it means you are important. God Himself made you this way and has a plan for your life, and your mission is to discover what that plan is. Obviously your part is important in the bigger picture of God's overall plan, or He wouldn't have created you.

It is frightening because it means that God is the only and final authority in everything. He is in charge of everything, and we are in charge of, well, nothing. The frightening part is that there are areas of our life where we are not bowing to His authority, but are demanding to be in charge.

As you sit reading this right now, you are in one of three groups of people.

The first group would be the people who claim there is no God. What they really mean is that there is no *one* God, but many. To some their god is their wealth, to some their power, to some their looks, to some their fame, to some their job, to some their spouse. The list could go on and on...hobbies, addictions, pleasures, treasures.

The focus of everything in their life is themselves. Everything else changes constantly because they are never satisfied with their latest "god" and need to find another one.

Purpose in life is fleeting, and hard to come by. It makes sense that it would be, given that they are here by accident, and that this accidental life is all there is. To them there is nothing after they die.

Live, die, that's it. Makes you kind of wonder why people work so hard to convince themselves that this is the way it is, doesn't it? It's not very appealing.

So why do they believe it?

They believe it because they insist on having the authority, and they will not submit to God's authority. And even as they deny that God exists, He has made it plain to them that He does.

And the reason their explanation for where we come from is so, to be honest, *lame* is because God's work in creation is so incredibly amazing in scope and detail. If you are in this group your unbelief about God and creation is not because of all the overwhelming evidence to the contrary. It is because of your unwillingness to submit your heart, and therefore your life, to the ultimate Authority.

If this group is right, life is all about chasing after happiness and meaning, but never getting it for long, and never finding fulfillment.

If they are wrong, they have spent their whole life spitting in the face of the God who created them, and whose authority they never acknowledged.

The second group is a large one.

These are the people who believe in God, and who believe that He created everything, but who misunderstand who He is because they have never gotten to know Him personally.

To a certain degree, this is understandable, because it is a lot more convenient to define God not by who He has revealed Himself to be, but by how you would like Him to be.

You know what I mean, don't you?

A God who is present and active when we want Him, and absent when we don't.

A God who is perfectly loving and merciful, but not so perfectly just.

A God who blesses, but never disciplines.

A God who does things for us so that we don't have to learn how to do them.

A God who is holy and perfect, but who will overlook our sins.

A God who is in authority on some things, and grants us authority on other things.

A God who changes with the times as our society "evolves" and "emerges".

A God who pays attention to you individually only when you need Him.

The truth is, if you look into the words He gave us in His book, the Bible, you will gain a different understanding of who God is, and it will change your life.

This is the part people in the second group hope to avoid, the changing the life part. Changing your life can get pretty inconvenient.

But it is the key to beginning to make sense of your life.

I think about how God reveals Himself in the Bible sometimes as I read it. It is really amazing when you think about it. He has **all** knowledge, and yet these are the words He has chosen for us to read. The Bible seems like a long book until you realize that of all the things He could teach us, this is what He gave us. He edited it down to what we could understand.

God has revealed Himself as our Father, and as a perfect Father He does what a perfect Father would do.

He is present and active all the time.

He is loving, merciful, *and* just.

He blesses, and He disciplines.

He helps us to continually grow and learn.

He does not overlook our sins.

He is in authority on all things.

He does not change.

He pays attention to you personally and individually all the time.

If you believe that He created you individually, that He crafted you to be exactly the way you are, then you have to know that He is there with you every step of the way through your life, and He is interested in your every move, every thought, every action... every moment of every day.

Pretty awesome, huh?!

It is hard for people in this second group to think about this, because it is a lot more attention from God than they would necessarily like. There are parts of their life where they would prefer His absence, especially where they know they are well outside of His moral law.

And here we are, back to the choice, like a fork in the road. Do we make the changes that truly giving Him authority in all things would require, and thus begin to make sense of our life? Or do we continue to seek Him when we need Him, and try to keep our life convenient but without much, if any, purpose?

The truth is we need Him all the time. He made us that way.

The third group is made up of people who acknowledge God as their Creator, and to whom He is the ultimate authority in every facet of their lives.

They are not perfect, and they are certainly not the judge of everyone else.

They have simply recognized that they belong to Him, and that His will is far more important than their own.

These are also not people for whom everything goes well all the time. God tests them, He disciplines them, He gives them battles to fight, He allows difficulties to help them to grow.

But He is always there for them, and they know it.

And they understand that whatever is going on in their life, it still has meaning because it is part of the plan their Creator has for them, a plan far greater than they can fathom. They know that since they are a part of His plan, they are important, and they commit themselves to doing their part for Him, their great Creator and ever-present Friend.

And in that there is joy, and life begins to make sense.

Where did *you* come from?

Until you answer that question truthfully, your life will never make sense.

# Chapter 2

# SHAPE

"So God created man in his own image,
in the image of God he created him;
male and female he created them."

Genesis 1:27

"When I consider your heavens,
the work of your fingers,
the moon and the stars,
which you have set in place,
what is man that you are mindful of him,
the son of man that you care for him?
You made him a little lower than the heavenly beings
and crowned him with glory and honor."

Psalm 8:3-5 ·

Malls and airports are great places for people watching. If you've ever sat in the middle of a mall waiting for someone you were with to get done shopping, or if you have ever sat in an airport waiting interminably for a flight (and who hasn't?) you know what I mean.

It's too busy and noisy and distracting to do much of anything else, so you watch all the people busily making their way to wherever they are going.

And you just have to marvel, don't you? Talk about your diversity! There are people of every imaginable age and color and attire and body language...and shape.

And part of what you do when you watch them, and don't try denying this because you know it's true, is to compare yourself to them.

You're better looking than some, thinner than some, younger than some.

And oh yes, you're also not as good-looking as some, heavier than some, and older than some.

So I doubt whether you've stood up on a bench or chair and announced to everyone in a very loud voice something like this:

"I have been looking at all of you, and I have now realized that I am without a doubt the most perfect creation God ever came up with."

No, I think it's safe to say that when you look in the mirror you don't see perfection.

Now, some of the imperfection is your own fault. If you eat too much and never exercise, you are likely to get overweight. If you don't brush your teeth they are going to look yellow instead of white. If you never get your hair trimmed from time to time it will probably go in some direction that doesn't enhance your appearance.

But outside of those kinds of things, you look like you do, and are shaped as you are, because God created you that way.

And He did it on purpose!

So you see you really are a perfect creation, and for two reasons.

The first reason is that God created you in His own image.

Now this does not mean that your physical appearance is that of God. We know that because we all look so different, and yet we are all created in the image of God. The image of God has to do with the inner shape, and that we will talk about later.

But you have to admit, it is very cool to be created in the image of God.

The second reason is that God created you to look like you do because you have a very specific and important purpose in his plan, and your role in his plan requires you to be shaped the way you are.

One of the great joys of life is discovering more and more about what your purpose is, and what His plan is for you, and how your shape fits into that plan. In a lifetime of seeking these answers, we generally only get a few, but there is as much joy in the *journey* of discovery as in the discovery itself.

Some things are obvious when you think about them.

For example, you know, don't you, that if you were stunningly beautiful or handsome that you might get a little conceited and self-centered. It would cause your inner shape to be less attractive if your outer shape was more attractive. I know you're telling yourself it wouldn't be so for *you*, but it would be.

Maybe some of your physical features, like your slightly too large nose, or that mole, or that double chin, or those thick legs, or those wrinkles, are there to keep you humble and to keep your focus on what is important.

If your looks are not that great, they are not as likely to become the focus of your life.

But if you are not careful, they could be.

We live in a world obsessed by outward appearance, by outer shape. It is in so many areas of our society the way people are measured.

So because we want to be admired, we start to think that changing our shape for the better will accomplish that. In so many marketing campaigns, that is the message. A lot of products are sold because people believe that if they are more beautiful or handsome, if they are thinner or more muscular, if they can cover every imperfection, they will have greater value.

This is an affliction for which there is only one cure: a recognition that God, the all-powerful, all-knowing God, created you exactly this way and considers you, just as you are, perfect for His plan.

Let's face it, the only way you can look at yourself and say that your outer shape is perfect is to acknowledge the truth that God in all His wisdom made you this way. Your value comes from God, the Creator of you.

And lest you start to believe that all of your physical qualities come from your parents or grandparents, consider the ways that you are *different* from your family.

God is very gracious in this way. I know this because He did not give me my great-grandfather's ears.

My great-grandfather, whose name was Charlie Brown (I'm not joking, it really was!), had very, very large ears. I'm talking very large. God's grace comes in at this point because Charlie's children had slightly smaller ears, and their children smaller yet, and by the time it got to me everybody's ears were normal size.

I don't know whether having large ears bothered my great-grandfather, as we never talked about it, and you can bet I wasn't going to bring it up, but if it *had* bothered him, would it have made his ears any smaller?

Of course not.

Now in today's world you can have all kinds of surgeries to try to change the way God created you, but you will still never be satisfied with the way you look until you look in the mirror and accept yourself the way He made you.

It's more than accepting, really. It's a matter of value. God created you the way He did for a reason, and you have value to Him. If you have value to God, you do Him a dishonor when you de-value yourself, when you try to improve on His work.

You are who you are because He wanted you this way. Isn't that absolutely *great*?!

Which brings us to the other part of your shape...your inner shape.

This is the part of us created in the image of God.

Just as we all have certain body parts in our outer shape, we also have certain parts to our inner shape: a soul, a conscience, a personality.

And just as our outer parts are shaped differently from one another, so are our inner parts. Some have more humility, some are quieter, some have more compassion, some more confidence, some more joy, and all with different talents and inner passions.

But where we start with our shape and where we finish are always going to be different.

Just as we need to accept and value our outer shape, and recognize its source, Almighty God, we need to do the same for our inner shape, for He has created that, as well.

Just as we can tone up our outer shape, we can also tone up our inner shape.

Just as our outer shape is affected by outside influences and people and experiences, so also is our inner shape.

And just as our outer shape was created by God to fulfill His purpose and demonstrate His glory, so also our inner shape is what it is because He wanted it that way as a part of His perfect plan.

If we try to change it, rather than seek to understand how He can use it for our joy and His glory, we dishonor Him, our Creator.

If we try to be someone we are not to make ourselves look good, whether our outer or inner shape, we are going to struggle to make sense of our life. If we try to use all the wonderful qualities and talents and passions He gave us to do our part in His plan, we will never doubt that we, and our life, have value.

And our life will make sense.

When I was in high school I worked for the local newspaper in my hometown in Minnesota. I realized at some point that if I was on the basketball team, I'd probably sit on the bench most of the time, but if I worked for the newspaper covering the basketball games, I'd have a seat in the press row and get paid for being there. So I covered lots of games.

I still vividly remember a basketball player named Ronnie Davison. He played for Springfield High School, our greatest basketball rival. Davison was slight in build and not very tall, maybe 5'9". He didn't look like he'd give you much trouble on a basketball court, but boy, could that young man score.

You would think he would get a lot of shots blocked, since he took a lot of shots, but I never once saw it happen. He was so quick, and so accurate, and had so many moves that when he wanted to shoot he could and would. The basketball was like an extension of his hand and arm, and he could dribble down the floor faster than most guys could run without it.

He drove everyone at my school crazy, because he seemed every year to be the reason we didn't go farther in the tournament.

When you looked at his outer shape, you'd never know that he was a great basketball player, but with talent and dedication he was.

And then there's my friend Jan.

Jan is about 10 years younger than me, and seriously disabled. She can walk a little, and see a little, and can do a few things with her hands and arms, but is very limited.

Now I will admit to being amazed at what she can accomplish physically, given her limitations. She lives alone, and takes good care of herself, and does more than you would ever imagine she could.

But it is her inner shape that is truly amazing.

Her physical limitations are of little concern to her, because God created her with a tremendous heart and soul, and she has taken her inner shape and toned it to do her best to mesh perfectly with God's will, and His plan.

You would think that her physical problems would cause her to be angry at God, or at the very least to believe that when it comes to God and His plan, she has no part in it with her situation. You would think she would have nothing to contribute to the great plan of the mighty God Himself.

But nothing could be further from the truth and the reality of her life.

Jan is one of the most encouraging people I know. She can type, and for as long as I've known her types notes to people. She has a joy that sneaks into all her notes and her conversations...it is unmistakable.

She has recently discovered the computer and email, and now she will really be a force in communicating God's message of truth and hope.

The secret of her joy?

She has discovered a great deal of God's plan for her. She has begun to understand the value God places on her, and why He has shaped her the way He has. She has used the inner shape God gave her to glorify Him, her Creator.

When you look at her, you'd never guess she was a great Christian example, but with the gifts God has given her, and dedication to her Creator, and faith in His plan, she is.

Your Creator shaped you the way He did for a reason.

In that truth lies your value.

It is up to you to work with it to begin to understand your role in His plan.

And your life has meaning, and begins to make sense.

# Chapter 3

# DIRECTION

"For this God is our God for ever and ever;
He will be our guide even to the end."
                                    Psalm 48:14


"I will lead the blind by ways they have not
known, along unfamiliar paths I will guide
them; I will turn the darkness into light before
them and make the rough places smooth.
These are the things I will do:
I will not forsake them."
                                    Isaiah 42:16

It was not in my plan to be an actor.

Now lest you misunderstand, I am not an actor by profession. However, it was God's plan for me to do some acting as a way for me to both serve Him and glorify Him.

When I first realized that God wanted me to audition for a theater production the church was planning, I'll admit I was horrified. I broke out in the sweats just thinking about standing up in front of drama experts and acting out a part for them.

My nervousness was well-merited. I had never done anything like it before, nor did I have any desire or fantasy to do it.

Oh, and did I mention that I had no idea what I was doing?

So why, you are wondering, did I do it? Why did I put myself through it?

Simple...it was God's will.

It took me a while to figure that part out, but God knows how dense I can be and He made it very clear to me. Several of my friends confirmed that this was something that, like it or not, I must do to please God.

After the audition, which was every bit as traumatic as I had imagined, I went home and told my wife Jackie that it appeared that God wanted me to learn a lesson in humility. So you can imagine how absolutely stunned I was when my sister-in-law Tricia, who was directing the play, called me and told me I had been cast in a part.

I believe my exact words to her were, "Were you not paying attention?"

My next comment was something like this: "I certainly hope you are a good director, because I have no idea what I'm doing. You will have to tell me exactly what I am supposed to do."

Tricia responded, "You can do this. I will help you and show you what you need to do."

She actually seemed pleased that she would be directing someone who would do precisely what she wanted, and who would be adding none of his own interpretation.

As it turned out, the play went fine, and I did all right, too. I did exactly what Tricia directed me to do, and that was definitely the best course of action.

And so it is with you and I...and God.

Since we are created by God, and shaped by God, it isn't difficult to figure out that God has a direction planned for our life. We go into it with no experience, with no idea what we are doing, and sometimes pretty nervous about it.

But God is an awesome director, and He will guide us through all of our new experiences and uncharted territory.

So the best course of action is to follow His direction.

However, just as I had the option of following Tricia's direction or not, we each have the option of following God's direction for our lives...or not.

There are some people who never follow God's direction their entire lives. I don't know what that is like, but I would guess it would leave a person feeling pretty empty and without purpose, not to mention nervous, what with all the changes in direction you would have to make to avoid God.

But most people follow God's direction, knowingly or unknowingly, some of the time, and go their own way the rest of the time.

When you look back, it's pretty easy to see...not so easy looking in the present and the future.

There are three ways that we choose which direction to go next in our lives.

The first is that we make a proactive choice.

Choosing a direction in this manner is usually done based on what we enjoy doing or on what we would like to accomplish, and is rarely a decision made with much thought about the long-term consequences.

Although I wouldn't necessarily characterize this kind of choice as pleasure-seeking, it does tend to be a decision made based on what we like, or think we'd like, at the present time. Often as time goes on this kind of choice of direction tends to lose its appeal, and sometimes we even begin to wonder what we were thinking when we made the decision to pursue this direction.

It is also important to note that sometimes we make direction decisions based on what other people in our life want rather than what we would prefer. It's still a proactive decision, but one made to please someone else, either because of our love for them or their intimidating influence in our life. When we begin to doubt or regret the choice, we tend to blame the person who influenced our decision, rather than accept responsibility for the choice ourselves.

A perfect example of this is when a young person chooses the career their father or mother wishes for them rather than making that choice themselves. It usually ends up being a mistake.

My dad always wanted me to be either a minister or an electrician. I know now that neither were God's direction for me, but my original decision to go a different direction was based in my desire to do something that I wanted to do...and maybe something of a rebellion thing, as well.

I have to tell you honestly, though, that if I had tried to become an electrician it would have really been a disaster. I would have been electrocuted a long time ago. At some point even my dad had to admit that was true.

So you make this proactive choice of direction, and your feeling when you make it is "this is going to be great!"

And then it seems at some point you end up saying "this is not working out."

When you make proactive choices based on what pleases you at the time, you always seem to end up changing direction later, when that choice is not looking like such a good one.

The second way we choose a direction in our life is that we make a reactive choice.

Whatever circumstances or people come our way, well, we just go with the flow.

Although this is a somewhat shallow way to choose direction, it is a very common one. Someone we are close with chooses a particular way of life, and we choose the same thing. They choose a career, and we choose the same one. They fall into a particular lifestyle, and we do the same.

Or we meet a young woman or young man we like, and they want to get married, so we get married to them.

Or someone in our social circle buys a new car or a bigger house, so we buy a new car or a bigger house.

Or someone we know joins a church, so we join it, too.

I think you probably get the gist of what I'm illustrating, and you would probably have to admit that you yourself have made some pretty big decisions about certain directions in your life in just this way. A door opens in front of you, and the lure of that open door just draws you in, whether it's a good thing for you or not.

And make no mistake about it, sometimes it *is* a good thing. Often, though, it is not.

We have the freedom to make our own decisions and choose our own direction without any human influences, and since we have to live with the consequences of our decisions and direction, it makes sense that we would take the time to choose based solely on what is best for us.

But we don't always do that, do we?

Which brings us to the third way that people choose the direction for their life, the path that they will follow.

And it is the only way that will ever make sense.

We let God direct us.

Admittedly this is difficult at first. The reason it is difficult is because we have to really get to know God, really get close to Him, before we can get comfortable with stepping out in faith on the path that He has chosen for us.

It is only when we begin to develop an understanding of how wise and powerful and loving God is that we begin to grasp the concept that our direction in life, and our life itself, will only make sense when we follow His direction.

When I think about this, I always end up thinking about Abram in the Old Testament. Abram was a very wealthy man, with a very comfortable life, and he really had no need of anything and probably, therefore, no desire to change too much of anything.

But Abram loved God, and *knew* God, and when God told him to pack up everything and move, he did it.

The thing was, God didn't tell him *where* he was to move, just to pack up and get moving.

And he *still* did it!

You see, Abram knew that God had a plan for his life, and he knew that if he went in the direction God sent him, all would be well, because he knew God loved him and would use him in incredible ways that he could never imagine.

And boy, did He ever! And Abram's life, a life of following God's direction, made sense. And it fit into the big picture of God's plan not just for Abram and his family, but for all mankind.

It is really quite amazing to think that God looks at you and I individually and has worked out the direction He would like us to go. The difficulty we have getting our minds around this is exactly why we need to devote time to getting to know God. You and I fit perfectly into this gigantic puzzle, but we are only capable of understanding a little bit of it, and thus we have to learn to trust the One who created and shaped us to fit, and Who is leading us where He wants us to go.

And just like Abram, when we leave this earth, as we all will, we will have no idea of the impact our seemingly small part in God's big plan will have.

I know what you're thinking. You're thinking, "God doesn't talk to me, He doesn't write me a letter or an email, and I don't know what He wants me to do."

I am here to tell you, He does that and more. He *will* reveal to you what He wants you to do if you make the effort to get to know Him, and if you will listen.

First, you must accept His Son, Jesus Christ, as your personal Savior. You must ask for forgiveness of the sins that separate you from Him, and must accept His free gift of salvation made possible by the sacrifice of Jesus on the cross. At this point you belong to Him, and the clear lines of communication are wide open.

Second, you must desire to know His will, and you must open your mind and your heart to whatever He wants, and you will begin to develop an understanding of where he wants you to go.

Third, your decision to take a certain direction must be consistent with what you read in the Words He gave you, the Bible.

Fourth, you must pray for direction. You must ask Him to make it clear to you what He wishes you to do.

Fifth, you must listen to his phone calls, emails, letters, and conversations. Granted, they will come from other people, but they are one of the ways He communicates His desire for your life. Godly people are so often God's messengers.

Finally, you must make your decision and ask Him to stop you if it is the wrong one.

I have to tell you this, though. Often God's direction for your life is beyond your understanding at the moment, and often it is something you believe you have no ability to accomplish.

Not to worry...this is how God makes it clear that it is *His* power at work, not yours.

Last week, one of my Christian sisters called me and asked me to prayerfully consider doing something. As usual, it was something I had never done, and yet, something I knew God had prepared me to do.

She said, "I know this may be outside your comfort zone, but...."

I responded, "Everything God has ever directed me to do was outside my comfort zone, but He has always faithfully guided me through."

And in this case, as I prayerfully sought answers to what He wanted me to do, it became clear to me that it was not His will, and within days it became clear that He had a different and better plan.

As I write this chapter, we are going through very difficult economic times, and I know a lot of people who suddenly and unexpectedly are without a job.

Some of them, those who don't know God personally, are very afraid and worried. They are proactively out there looking for job security somewhere, anywhere, and who believe they will have to do this all on their own.

Some of them are waiting for something to come along, and whatever comes is the direction they will now go.

And some of them are turning to the God they know so well and love so much, seeking His guidance and direction, knowing that He is right there with His plan for their life and that whatever happens He will care for them. At the same time they are looking for work, they are looking for affirmation from God that if they find work it will be what He wishes them to do.

When the Creator of all things, the One who shaped you exactly the way you are, chooses your direction, you have nothing to worry about, for with Him all things are possible.

Doing exactly what God directs is definitely the best course of action.

Makes sense, doesn't it?

# Chapter 4

# PURPOSE

"Many are the plans in a man's heart,
but it is the Lord's purpose that prevails."
Proverbs 19:21

"However, I consider my life worth nothing to me, if only I may finish the race and complete the task the Lord Jesus has given me—the task of testifying to the gospel of God's grace."
Acts 20:24

"But one thing I do: Forgetting what is behind and straining toward what is ahead, I press on toward the goal to win the prize for which God has called me heavenward in Christ Jesus."
Philippians 3:13b-14

M y son Justin and I like to play ping pong. We have for a long time, 11 years to be precise.

I know this because we have lived in this house for 11 years, and right after we moved in here we bought a ping pong table and set it up in the basement.

Justin has never grown tired of playing ping pong. Even now, at age 19, every time he is here he asks me to play. I think that his reason now to play is different than it was years ago.

He is pretty sure that he is going to win.

He is usually right about that. He is a *very* good ping pong player.

To explain how this happened, I have to go back to when we first started playing. You see, I never played ping pong with him just to bounce the ball back and forth and keep it on the table.

I played to *win.*

Admittedly, a big part of my playing to win has to do with my competitive nature. But I also knew that if Justin learned how to compete and lose, he would be a better person for the experience.

I didn't think about it for a long time after we started playing each other, but at some point I realized that he had *never* beaten me in a single game. It frankly amazed me that he always wanted to play, and he never, ever won. I would estimate that I won about 2000 games in a row before he ever beat me.

But through that whole losing streak he learned. He discovered his weaknesses, and worked on them. He watched the types of shots, and the strategies, I used to beat him and started to work on those, as well. When his backhand was his weakness, I mercilessly pounded shot after shot at that backhand, and in the process I unknowingly made his backhand his best shot.

It also didn't hurt that he grew taller than me, and with long arms that made it very difficult to get a shot past him.

After all that losing one day he won a game. We both kind of knew it was a rather momentous occasion...and we both knew it was going to happen again.

And it did.

And now it happens most of the time. I always agree to play him every time he asks, even though I know I will probably lose, which I don't like doing. I owe him that, this kid who never quit playing and trying and learning, and who persevered through the longest losing streak in ping pong history.

Though we loved playing and competing, though it was fun and there were many weird and wild shots that made us laugh, we both had a purpose.

Justin's purpose was to win a game.

Mine was to win every game.

I think about this sometimes. If I had allowed him to win on occasion, or we just hit the ball back and forth, he would never be the ping pong player he is today. If he had given up and become tired of losing all the time, same result.

But we both had a purpose...a goal, if you will...and we never lost sight of it.

So it is with our life. If it has purpose, we grow, we learn, we persevere, and in that purpose we eventually and occasionally win.

Once we understand we are created by God and shaped by God, and once we are allowing God to direct our life, then He can give our life purpose.

It is tough to go through life with no purpose. I know people who live a life without purpose, who just plod on from day to day, doing this and doing that, and accomplishing nothing of consequence.

These are the unhappiest people I know. Most of them are kind of sad. Many of them could be called depressed.

They never get where they are going, because they are going nowhere.

And while they are accomplishing nothing, a purpose for their life exists, but remains unfulfilled.

Thankfully, there are not many of these people, although their numbers seem to be increasing as the Source of purpose, God Almighty, has been to a large degree expelled from modern society.

There are also people who go through their life trying to figure out their purpose, thinking that their life experiences are taking them through some kind of process toward a discovery of a monumental reason why they are here.

They are in a constant state of confusion and change, examining this and that experience in their life to see if it gives them a clue as to their purpose.

I'm not really sure, but it seems as if they are convinced that at some point very late in their life, everything that happened to them will now make sense, that it all had to do with this elusive purpose they've been trying to discover.

They seem to be pretty sure that this purpose is a pretty amazing thing, something that is, at least for the moment, beyond their understanding.

There are also people who believe that their life has lots of different purposes. They mistake the journey for the destination, so to speak. They think the process of fulfilling their purpose IS their purpose.

They think their purpose is to learn to hit a good backhand shot, when in fact learning to hit a good backhand shot is part of fulfilling their real purpose: becoming a great ping pong player.

Then they think their purpose is to learn to hit a good serve, when in fact that, too, is a part of fulfilling their real purpose of becoming a great ping pong player.

I will admit, these are interesting people. They have singular focus most of the time, and once they have reached their latest goal, they immediately zero in on a new one. It is absolutely fascinating to hear them answer the question "What's new?".

The truth is that we all, though we are vastly different in shape and direction, have one clear and distinct purpose: to make known to others who God is and what He has done for all of us.

Think about it. God created you in His own image. That means that you are able to *show* others who He is. The Bible says we are to "reflect" His glory, that the incredible light that He is should bounce off us and be seen by others in what we do and say.

It's even more incredible when you realize that He could show who He is and what He has done in an infinite number of amazing ways, including lots of ways we can't even begin to imagine.

But He chose to show other people who He is and what He has done through us.

Now that is some purpose.

The creative part comes from the fact that He shaped us all in different ways, inside and out, and directs us each in our individual ways, to accomplish the very same purpose. Thus we are effective in fulfilling our part of His greater plan because of how he shaped us and directs us.

Where we begin to struggle is when we get the *path* He has put us on to fulfill His purpose for us confused with the purpose itself.

We resolve this when we focus back on the purpose.

In order to effectively communicate to those around us who God is and what He has done for us, we have to know it ourselves. When we make knowing Him personally better and better every day a permanent part of our life, we are on the path to fulfilling our life's purpose.

Although God is evident in all we see around us, the incredible creation and how it works in perfect harmony, not to mention its beauty, we can best get to know Him by the Words that He has given us.

I am always amazed by the Bible. Every day I read some of it, and every day it changes me for the better. I think about all the days in my past when I did not read it, and can't help but wonder what I might have done for God if I had. I also understand, looking back at those days, that I was accomplishing very little, if anything, of my life's purpose because I had lost the message I was created to proclaim.

The Bible is perfection and power, encouragement and knowledge, the key to understanding why life makes sense. It is impossible to have purpose without it, because it contains what we need to fulfill our purpose.

It tells us, so that we can tell others, not only who God is but what He has done.

What kind of God, seeing the people He created making a mess of things, sends His only Son from heaven to this place, earth, to be mistreated and killed in order to save those disobedient and ungrateful people?

A God of love.

A God of mercy.

A God of grace.

That's the kind of God.

Since our purpose in life is to make that kind of God known, it is without a doubt the greatest purpose He could ever give us.

The other area where we struggle is in trying to understand how we fit into His greater plan, how our little part makes a difference in the big picture, how our being here could possibly matter.

My family almost always has a jigsaw puzzle going in the living room. We all like doing them, and we especially enjoy the feeling of acomplishment, not to mention the beautiful picture, when they are done.

Now of course when you work on a jigsaw puzzle, you always have the box there with the picture of what it will look like when it's all done. This is both a goal and a guide. If you had to put that puzzle together having never seen the big picture, it would be much more difficult.

God sees the big picture, and knows exactly where we fit in. We do not, and cannot, see what He sees. He allows us to see small sections of the big picture, the part we are capable of seeing and understanding, to encourage us to stay true to His purpose for our life.

I call these glimpses "doses of grace". Although I have experienced these many times in my life, I only began to understand them in the face of tragedy. Now I see them more clearly than I used to.

When we are not seeing the big picture, not understanding what difference we are making, that is where faith comes in.

And faith stays strong when we stay connected to the God who gave us this incredible purpose in life.

You know the God I mean, don't you?

The God who created us.

The God who shaped us.

The God who directs us.

The God who loves us.

The God who saved us.

That God.

Our purpose is to make known who He is and what He has done.

There is none greater.

# Chapter 5

# MEANING

"Meaningless! Meaningless!" says the Teacher. "Utterly meaningless!
Everything is meaningless."
What has been will be again, what has been done will be done again; there is nothing new under the sun.
I have seen all the things that are done under the sun;
all of them are meaningless, a chasing after the wind."

Ecclesiastes 1:1,9,14

"I know that everything God does will endure forever; nothing can be added to it and nothing taken from it. God does that so that men will revere Him."

Ecclesiastes 3:14

"Now all has been heard;
here is the conclusion of the matter:
Fear God and keep His commandments,
for this is the whole duty of man.
For God will bring every deed into judgment,
including every hidden thing
whether it is good or evil."

Ecclesiastes 12:13-14

"Why spend your money on what is not bread,
and your labor on what does not satisfy?
Listen, listen to me, and eat what is good, and
your soul will delight in the richest of fare."
Isaiah 55:2

I was only a basketball coach for one season, and it was a long time ago, but I will never forget it.

I was in the Army, stationed in West Berlin in 1972. I worked in what the Army called Special Services. I worked out of the Tours Office, giving tours mostly of East Berlin but also West Berlin.

I knew this lieutenant in Special Services who was in charge of something called AYA, which stood for American Youth Association. He set up and coordinated activities for the children of American military personnel stationed in West Berlin.

They had a fifth grade boys' basketball league that was just getting ready to start their season, and they had a better turnout than expected, and thus were in need of one more coach. The lieutenant, whose name was Mike, asked me if I would be willing to coach a team.

This sounded really good to me. I loved basketball and knew a lot about the sport, and was very competitive. I thought it would be fun to make future NBA stars out of these boys.

What Mike did *not* tell me was that all the other teams had been formed via a draft, in which the coaches picked the players one by one, and that I had all the kids who had not been picked... by anyone.

Well, you can imagine how good we were. These boys tried hard and were very coachable, but we were blown out in our first two games. We all pretty much resigned ourselves to just learning and having fun.

Then a new kid whose dad had just been assigned to West Berlin joined our team. Apparently since we were the last team the first newcomer went to us. Well, as it turns out, this boy was a terrific basketball player, and he fit right in with the rest of the team, and the next thing you know everyone was playing better.

We began to believe that we could actually win a game, and our season started taking on new meaning.

Then we *did* win a game, and now the boys were beginning to believe.

However, our next game was against the best team in the league. They were the best team because they had the best player. He was 6'2" tall (yes, in the 5$^{th}$ grade!) and very coordinated, not to mention skilled.

We had a meeting to discuss this game. It was interesting. No, it was amazing. I looked into the eyes of these boys and realized they believed they were going to beat a team that had won every game by 20 points or more. There wasn't a lot of strategy discussed at this meeting, but there was a lot of fist-pumping and high-fiving.

I, being an adult, was skeptical, but I stuck to coaching. I didn't want them to lose their enthusiasm. They were absolutely jazzed, and having fun.

Well, you guessed it. We won the game. Although three of my players fouled out guarding this big kid, he got so frustrated by how intensely they guarded him that he also fouled out, and his team turned out not to be so good without him.

I have never seen greater determination to this day than those boys exhibited that day. And when I looked again into the eyes of those boys after we won that game, I saw more than joy. I saw fulfillment.

I know you're thinking we went undefeated the rest of the way and won the championship of the league. No, sorry, this isn't a movie, though that one game would have made a great one. We only lost a couple of games in the regular season, and we lost in the semi-finals of the tournament.

But oddly enough, that team never lost what had been discovered, even in defeat.

The team, the games, the season had meaning.

And so it is with each one of us. We can do satisfying or even pleasurable things, we can enjoy some type of activity, we can find a career or house or spouse that we really love, but we want, and need, more.

Life, to be fulfilling and to make sense, needs meaning.

Once you understand that God created us this way it is a lot easier to find the meaning. He meant for us to be this way, so that He could provide the meaning.

Meaning is different than purpose. Purpose is more like a goal, a place we want to go, something we are reaching for.

Meaning is now and every moment, an affirmation that what we are doing right now is important. It is a source of ongoing motivation.

There is no such thing as temporary meaning. That is why there is no meaning in life without God.

Oh, it has been, and continues to be tried without God, but He has created us in such a way that we will never find meaning without a relationship, a personal relationship, with Him.

The amazing part is that He does not force us to do this (like we would do if WE were God). He gives us the freedom to live our life with meaning (with Him as our focus) or without meaning (without Him).

You see, the truth is still the truth, whether we acknowledge it or not.

God created each of us and thus is the ultimate authority in life (the truth), yet He allows us to, if we wish, live our life in denial of His authority.

God shaped us each individually the way He did for a reason (the truth), yet He allows us to believe and live as if we are an accident or coincidence.

God has a specific direction for our life (the truth), yet He allows us to pick whatever direction we wish, and to change it as often as we like.

God has given each one of us purpose by way of the shape and direction He has for us (the truth), yet He will not stop you if you want to flail around blindly and try to find it on your own.

God gives our life meaning if we simply honor and obey Him (the truth), yet He will allow you to dishonor and disobey Him, and live a life without meaning, if you choose.

But for everything you do that defies God, for every time you deny truth, there is a price you must pay, both now in this life and later in the next.

I cannot talk about meaning in life without talking about the book of Ecclesiastes. If you have never read this book in the Bible, you need to read it. If you have read it before, even if you have read it many times, you need to read it again. In fact, you need to read it no later than the end of this chapter.

The book of Ecclesiastes was written by Solomon, the son of David, and a man who was unquestionably one of the greatest kings of all time. Solomon had everything, and I do mean everything, in this life. He had the things many people seek: wealth, power, wisdom and popularity.

There was nothing Solomon wanted in this life that he couldn't have...nothing.

And yet he found his life without meaning.

He sought meaning in every aspect of life, since he had the means to do so.

He sought meaning in pleasure, he sought it in wealth, he sought it in power, he sought it in other people's admiration, he sought it in wisdom.

But he didn't find it there.

He found it in God, specifically in honoring and obeying God.

He learned it the hard way and wrote it all down so we wouldn't have to experience the frustration of living life without meaning, life without God.

And yet, for the 3,000 years or so that have passed since he wrote the book, people are continuing to make the same mistakes he did.

My guess is that your life is not completely without meaning. Few people are in that terrible place.

But oddly enough, those few people may be closer to finding the answer than you are. They are in such a desperate situation, feel so lost and alone, and are so painted into a corner that they are turning to God. For them perhaps there is nowhere else to turn.

And when they do, He is right there waiting. He never gives up on anyone. His grace is so amazing that He will reveal to those who call on Him how to find meaning in their life.

Most people aren't in that position, though. Most people find some meaning in some parts of their life because in those parts they *do* honor and obey God. They have perhaps just never made the connection between meaning and God.

Or maybe they have, but have only allowed God into certain parts of their life because they are unwilling to give up something that gives them pleasure, or wealth, or other people's admiration, or power.

You know, those things that have no meaning, those things Solomon tried.

Yet they will continue to find that those things that they won't give to God, those areas of life where they won't submit to God, won't honor and obey Him, will continue to leave them empty and unfulfilled.

In a word, meaningless.

It requires us to change to get on the path God has for us, something we resist on a regular basis, but it is on that path that we will find meaning.

Ironic, isn't it?

The part that should concern each one of us, for ourselves and for those we love, is that God will bring everything to justice in the end. In Solomon's conclusion to Ecclesiastes he says that God will bring every deed into judgment, whether good or evil, even the things that are hidden to other people.

Though God gives us the freedom to deny the truth, the freedom to deny His existence as Creator and Authority, the freedom to seek our own direction and purpose, He will someday call us before Him to answer to all this, and He will judge us.

The most amazing thing about God, though, is that through His grace and mercy He has given us a way to stand before Him on that day spotless, our sins covered by the blood of His Son, Jesus Christ, whose sacrifice on our behalf makes this possible.

Once we acknowledge that sacrifice, and accept His gift of grace, not only are we spared from a terrible judgment, but we are empowered by Him to change the areas of our life that had no meaning, to shed the burden they have become, and to move our life toward honoring and obeying Him in everything.

Then everything in our life has meaning.

Recently a young lady was talking to me about the futility of her life. She didn't especially like her job, she was struggling financially, she was in conflict with her mother, and her relationship with her boyfriend was something of a mess. As she was talking about this, she began to cry, and I could see that she was suffering because her life was without direction, purpose, or meaning.

I gently told her that her Creator, Almighty God, held the answer for everything that was troubling her.

And though her initial reaction was that this was not what she wanted to hear, I could see in her tear-filled eyes that she knew it was true.

I also knew at that moment that this suffering, this life with no meaning that she was going through, was necessary for her to experience to turn to the God that loves her beyond all her understanding.

Perhaps you are suffering in some areas of your life, too.

If so, I'm here to tell you, too, that your Creator, God Almighty, holds the answer for everything that troubles you.

Perhaps you, too, do not want to hear this, but I know that you, too, your eyes full of tears, know it is true.

There is no meaning in life without God.

If you honor and obey Him, He will give you meaning, and victories, you never could have imagined.

He will never give up on you, either. He's always right there, waiting to fill your life with meaning.

Though you will not win every game, you will never forget when your life began to have meaning.

# Chapter 6

# INTENTION

"I do not understand what I do. For what I want to do I do not do, but what I hate to do. And if I do what I do not want to do, I agree that the law is good. As it is, it is no longer I myself who do it, but it is sin living in me. I know that nothing good lives in me, that is, in my sinful nature. For I have the desire to do what is good, but I cannot carry it out. For what I do is not the good I want to do; no, the evil I do not want to do—this I keep on doing. Now if I do what I do not want to do, it is no longer I who do it, but it is sin living in me that does it."

Romans 7:15-20

"For the Word of God is living and active. Sharper than any double-edged sword, it penetrates even to dividing soul and spirit, joints and marrow; it judges the thoughts and attitudes of the heart. Nothing in all creation is hidden from God's sight. Everything is uncovered and laid bare before the eyes of him to whom we must give account."

Hebrews 4:12-13

"There is a way that seems right to a man, but in the end it leads to death."

Proverbs 14:12

I was going to be a newspaper publisher.

However, I am not now, and never have been, and I'm guessing never will be, a newspaper publisher. That is probably a good thing, since newspapers are becoming a thing of the past.

But I did intend, as a young man, to be a newspaper publisher. In high school and my first year of college I worked for my hometown newspaper, and in the course of six years I did pretty much everything on the editorial side of the newspaper. I covered sports events and city council meetings, I wrote news stories of all kinds, from obituaries to features, I wrote editorials on occasion, and even edited the paper itself at times.

It was as great a part-time and summer job as any kid has ever had, in my opinion. I absolutely loved it.

So it was natural for me to develop a desire to be a newspaper publisher some day.

A lofty goal, I believed.

The ultimate prize, I thought.

But it never happened, because at some point I realized that this was not what I wanted to do for a career. I involved myself one summer on the "business" side of the newspaper, selling advertising space, and though I did well enough at it, it fell far short of being fulfilling.

I *intended* to become a newspaper publisher, but never did.

Now I am a financial advisor, something I never intended to be, but a profession that God clearly chose for me years ago. I must admit that He made a good choice, and I'm glad that I followed His guidance.

Having the *intention* of being a publisher did not make it happen. I would have had to actually carry it through. I never did.

And so it is with much of our lives. We have an intention of doing something or being something or changing something, and we never do it.

Why is this? Well, it's in our nature.

When God created man and woman, Adam and Eve, at first everything was perfect. That's right, *perfect*. The relationship between God and his creation was perfectly harmonious.

And God only had one (yes, only one!) law.

And Adam and Eve broke that one law.

They sinned...against God, their Creator.

And the perfect relationship was no more.

We have inherited the sinful nature that began with Adam and Eve. We may desire and intend to do good and obey God's laws, but we do not. It is not in our nature, not since Adam and Eve broke that one law.

I have heard many people say, and I'm sure you've heard it as well, that man is "basically good". I have no idea how anyone who looks around them could ever come to that conclusion. They are in the worst and most dangerous kind of denial.

You and I are born with a sinful nature, one that causes us to regularly violate God's laws.

That sinful nature has also separated us from God, because God, in His perfection, cannot and will not tolerate sin and imperfection.

And only God, in His perfection, could make a way for us to be not only cleansed from the filthiness of our sin, but to be *changed* from a sinful nature to a Godly nature, and thus to be allowed in His presence for all eternity.

Which is exactly what our loving, amazing God did.

You and I know that the best intentions have never accomplished anything. It's only a matter of time until those great intentions are abandoned in some self-serving compromise.

Often, too, we have so many good intentions that we never carry out any of them.

Recently I was talking to a young man who was complaining about his uncle. I know his uncle fairly well myself. He is a very likable man who has many great things he would like to accomplish, and will readily tell you about these goals. He is so outgoing and enthusiastic that it sometimes causes people to question his sincerity.

That is what was happening with his nephew. The young man said "I just don't trust him."

I explained to the young man that his uncle is not unworthy of his trust, but is simply one of those people who has 400 great ideas today, zeroes in on two or three of them, and then the next day forgets them all and has 400 more great ideas.

In other words his intentions are good, and his accomplishments are few. He is an airplane that never comes in for a landing.

You know people like that, too, don't you?

You can have nothing but good intentions, but you still have that sinful nature, and you will not carry many of them out.

This is where we have to go back and recap.

If you understand that God is your Creator, then you know that He is the ultimate authority in your life.

And as such, it is *His* intention that we need to carry out.

Ours may be good, but His is perfect...and perfectly fitted for us.

Not only that, but He will empower us to carry it out.

This is where we often have an issue. We know God is the ultimate authority, but we so often go off on our own way and do not defer to His authority.

We see this pretty often in our society today. We are in lockstep with God's laws and the instructions in His Word for some things, but over time we start compromising more and more, either to try to alleviate guilt over something we do, or to convince ourselves that He will not condemn someone we love for what they are doing.

But once we submit ourselves to His authority, we begin to appreciate and understand why He shaped us the way He did.

Once we submit to His authority, we begin to figure out the direction He has chosen for our lives, and the wisdom of that direction.

Once we submit to His authority, we have purpose every day and in everything we do, a purpose about which we keep learning more and more.

Once we submit to His authority, our life takes on deep meaning.

And perhaps most importantly, once we submit to His authority and trust Him in all things, we are increasingly comfortable with the truth that He knows our intentions, what is in our heart, and He will help us to carry out those intentions that honor Him.

Now I have been assuming all along that you have good intentions. Certainly if you are reading this book that would be a logical assumption.

And I have been focusing on having good intentions, but lacking the nature to carry them out.

God knows about your good intentions, and He has made a way for you to put aside your sinful nature and carry them out.

But understanding that we are born with a sinful nature also means that we are going to have some bad intentions, as well.

It would be more accurate to call them *evil* intentions, really.

"Not me!" you exclaim in protest.

But it's true, isn't it?

Not only do we sometimes act in dishonest, unethical, unkind, and immoral ways, but most of the time we *intend* to do so in advance.

We attempt to justify these intentions and actions by proclaiming our victimhood, or our rights, or our importance, or our superiority in morals or intellect.

God, who is supreme in authority, knows about these bad intentions as well, even when we don't carry them out.

And we are right back at the sinful nature, aren't we?

God did create you. If you do not believe that, you are in the worst kind of trouble, in danger of eternal torment. Your sinful nature will keep you separated from His presence forever. You need to challenge that selfish and shallow kind of thinking, or stand condemned before Him some day.

But if you do believe that God created you, you need to submit to His authority, not just to save yourself from eternal death in the future, but to have a joyful and meaningful life in the present.

So how can a person with a sinful nature, and who, despite their best intentions, keeps violating God's laws ever cleanse themselves so they can stand in the presence of their Creator?

It's simple...and it's free.

It's called grace.

God knew we could never do it on our own, so He made a way. He sent His own Son down from the glory of heaven to earth to live a sinless life, then to die as a sacrifice for the forgiveness of our sins. Then He raised Him from the dead to reign as our Lord and Savior forever.

How do you get rid of the sin that separates you from God, and how do you change from that sinful nature to a holy and Godly nature?

You accept the free gift of grace. You acknowledge what God and His Son, Jesus Christ, did for you. You surrender your meaningless life to Him, and He will give you new life, a meaningful life.

You say it in words, out loud, in private. Just Him and you. You tell him you are sorry for all your sinful intentions and actions, and that you want to be cleansed of your sin so that you can be with Him for eternity when this life is over. You commit yourself to His will, understanding that His will for your life is perfect, just as in all things He is perfect. You acknowledge that Jesus is now Lord of your life, and that you are trusting Him to save you.

Your life will then be profoundly changed. You will never be the same, and you will forever recognize it as the single most important day of your life.

You will not be *instantly* transformed into a Godly nature. It is a process, and it will take time as you develop both your relationship with Jesus and your trust in Him.

But every sin you commit from that day forward, every evil intention and action, will be forgiven when you ask God to forgive it in Jesus' name.

And you will stand before Him some day whiter than new fallen snow, perfectly sinless in His presence.

You cannot do this on your own. With the best of intentions, you still have a sinful nature.

And you do not have to try to do this on your own.

He has made a way.

I don't know about you, but I am way beyond awe that he loves me that much.

# Chapter 7

# DISTRACTION

"For all have sinned and fall short of the glory of God."

Romans 3:23

"The Lord is gracious and compassionate,
slow to anger and rich in love.
The Lord is faithful to all his promises
and loving toward all he has made.
The Lord upholds all those who fall
and lifts up all who are bowed down."

Psalm 145:8, 13b-14

"If the Lord delights in a man's way,
he makes his steps firm;
though he stumble he will not fall,
for the Lord upholds him with his hand."

Psalm 37:23-24

Afew years ago I learned an important lesson about ladders. I was painting the outside of my house. It needed it, and we had picked out a different color that we preferred over the color it was when we bought the house.

Now although I am not, generally speaking, very handy, I am pretty good at painting, and I was breezing along and it was looking pretty good. I painted the lower parts using a stepladder, because you could set the can of paint on the little platform on the ladder, and you could cover quite a bit before having to move the ladder. Plus the stepladder was pretty solid if you set it on level ground.

When I got to the higher parts, though, I had to use an extension ladder. This meant holding the can of paint, and it meant moving the ladder pretty often, as it was harder to reach much area. And, of course, the ladder, being extended pretty far, was a lot shakier to stand on.

Now all of you reading this probably know that you need to anchor the feet of that extension ladder very solidly, even perhaps putting something heavy at the base of it to keep the feet from sliding out and the ladder falling. I guess I knew that, too, but in my haste to get the job done I didn't really do that. I moved the ladder to the next spot, set the feet down as solidly as possible, and scampered up to the top.

You can probably also guess what happened. I was at the highest point of the ladder and the house, and the feet slid out away from the house, and down went the ladder...and me with it.

It was kind of like in the cartoons, when the character runs off the cliff, hangs in the air, looks at the camera, says "uh-oh", and then falls. It seemed to me like the ladder fell, then I realized what had happened, and then I fell.

The ladder fell about 15 feet (as did I) and landed on a bush directly below. I came down on my shin bone on the frame of the ladder, bounced off, and fell the rest of the way to the ground.

My first thought was that I must have broken my leg. I jumped up to see if I could walk, and when I realized I could, felt pretty sure I hadn't broken anything, although the pain coming from my leg told me that whatever I *had* done was probably not good. Then my son, who was painting window trim in the same area, came over looking horrified and pointing at my forearm. I looked at the arm and discovered I had gashed it on the bush, and had blood, paint, dirt, and parts of the bush pretty much everywhere.

As it turned out, the arm looked worse than it was, and once I got it cleaned up and bandaged it was obviously going to be okay, though I would certainly have a scar. The muscles in front of my shin bone where I had landed on the ladder frame had knotted up in a tight little ball (I'm told this is what they do to protect you), but there appeared to be no permanent or serious damage.

But I will tell you this: I did no more painting that day. I guess you could say I was a little distracted.

And when I did resume painting a couple of days later, I anchored the extension ladder with a very heavy planter, *and* had my wife Jackie hold the base of that ladder. Not only that, but I painted a little tiny section (NO reaching!) and then very, very carefully came down and moved the ladder to the next location.

Truth be told, my legs were pretty shaky going up and down that ladder, and I was very relieved when the high parts were done.

And so it is with life.

We are cruising along, and all is going well. We are confident, we feel like we are on the right path, and we are accomplishing a lot. We may even be following God's direction and purpose for our life.

And then comes that distraction. Then comes the fall.

And suddenly we're not so excited about "painting". We have other things that we now have to deal with.

And we are off the path we were so confidently following.

You have to understand first of all that there are two kinds of distractions.

The first kind is the distraction that we either choose or fall into because of our carelessness.

We become somewhat obsessed by something or someone, and it begins to dominate our life and takes us off the path we were on, and the next thing you know we have fallen and we are lost.

This can be a person, a job, a hobby, or money. It can be an illness that we choose to allow to dominate us rather than keep it in its place. It can be as simple as television, or video games, or the computer, or even sports.

But whatever this distraction is, it not only changes our direction in life, it also changes the kind of person we are becoming. We are changing, but we are not growing. We are not moving forward, but are either moving sideways or backward.

Nearly always this kind of distraction, this straying from the path that God has laid out for us, happens because of our overconfidence.

We trust in ourselves and our ability rather than in God, and this makes us susceptible to falling, to seeking fulfillment by our own power or allowing something that has unexpectedly come into our life to change us.

Self-fulfillment or self-pity.

And it can be hard to get up from a fall like that.

It is very important to realize that prior to a fall like that, a distraction if you will, there is first temptation. This temptation is the work of one who wishes for your death, who yearns for your total destruction, and who will use your weaknesses against you if you allow it.

His name is Satan. And yes, he does exist.

But one day *he* will be destroyed.

He would like to take you with him, but God can save you from him.

Jesus dealt with Satan in the most effective way, and thus showed us how to do it. When Jesus was tempted by Satan, he used God's words from the Scriptures to repel this sworn enemy of God.

We can do the same thing. If we are focused on the words God gave us in the Bible on a regular basis, we are continually empowered to fight off the temptations, and therefore the fall that we might otherwise take.

If you look at your life, and what you are trusting in yourself alone to do and accomplish, you will find that this is where the next potential distraction lies. This is where the danger exists that you will take off on a path not chosen by God. This is where you might fall off the ladder.

There is, after all, in these areas of great confidence in yourself, no anchor.

The second kind of distraction is a divine one.

God sometimes puts you "on the sidelines" for a time as part of His purpose for your life.

This makes sense when you understand that God is Supreme over everything and everyone, Everything that happens to you is either something He has made happen, or that He has allowed to happen.

When tragedy or trouble or trial comes into your life, He is aware of it.

When you fall, He knows about it.

When you are stopped in your tracks from what has become "normal" for you in your life, He understands all about it.

Which means He either allowed it, or He orchestrated it for your good.

The hard part about this is trying to understand why God has allowed or put this distraction in your life. It may, though, be a long time before we are able to understand the greater purpose He has, and it may even be that we never totally understand it.

That is where faith comes in.

He wants you to trust Him.

This is actually easier to do than you might think. If you believe that God created you, shaped you and directs you, and if you believe that He has a purpose for your life, and if you believe that He will give your life meaning, then you know enough about Him to be able to trust Him.

Some of the distractions He sends our way are so that we will learn something. I know I learned how to properly use an extension ladder after I fell.

Some of them may be to help get us back on the path He has for us, as we may be starting to stray just a little. I know I had gotten a little overconfident and in too big of a hurry while I was painting.

Some of them may be to build our faith in Him. I know I prayed a prayer of thanks after I fell off the ladder, because I knew He had kept me from being seriously injured.

Some of them may be for the benefit of other people. For all I know, I fell off the ladder so that I could write this chapter years later and have it make sense to you.

Some of them are meant to "paint us into a corner" so that we will turn to Him and surrender our lives to Him.

I have a friend with whom I have lunch fairly often. I talk to him about spiritual things, which is quite normal for me, and he is fascinated by it. It amazes him that we, two guys, are sitting there talking about deep and important truths. But this man, about whom I care deeply, stubbornly refuses to let God into his life. In fact, you might say he carefully avoids having any personal contact with God.

I often tell him that God is very close to him whether he likes it or not, and yet that the next step is up to him. I also warn him that God may bring something into his life that will cause him to make contact, something not so good.

Last time we had lunch I told him I was thinking about praying that God would bring a trial into his life so that he would turn to God. He looked shocked, and said to me "Don't do that!".

And yet I wonder if that is not what it will take...a distraction that makes him aware of the presence and wonder and love and grace of his Creator.

I probably shouldn't have said it, because if God does "paint him into a corner" he will think I caused it to happen. But I care about him, and know that his life will become a joyful one if he turns it all over to God.

It's also true that some of the distractions that God puts in our life give us great joy. He may put a special person or a special project (like writing a book for Him!) in our life for a time, something that especially blesses us.

The key to understanding the kind of distraction that is going on in our life is in our relationship with God. If we understand God's supremacy, and if we are close enough to Him to understand His direction and purpose in our life, we will know whether what has caused us to stumble and fall is our own doing or His.

Then we will know how we must handle it. In that knowledge lies the key to how it affects us, and how we react to it.

Romans 8:28 says, "And we know that in all things God works for the good of those who love him, who have been called according to his purpose."

And in that our life, no matter what comes our way, makes sense

# Chapter 8

# ACTION

"What good is it, my brothers, if a man claims to have faith but has no deeds?
Can such faith save him? Suppose a brother or sister is without clothes and daily food. If one of you says to him, "Go, I wish you well; keep warm and well fed," but does nothing about his physical needs, what good is it? In the same way, faith by itself, if it is not accompanied by action, is dead. But someone will say,
"You have faith; I have deeds." Show me your faith without deeds, and I will show you my faith by what I do. You believe that there is one God. Good!
Even the demons believe that - and shudder. As the body without the spirit is dead, so faith without deeds is dead."

James 2:14-19,26

"You are the light of the world. A city on a hill cannot be hidden.
Neither do people light a lamp and put it under a bowl. Instead they put it on its stand, and it gives light to everyone in the house. In the same way, let your light

shine before men, that they may see your good deeds and praise your Father in heaven."

Matthew 5:14-16

"And whatever you do, whether in word or deed, do it all in the name of the Lord Jesus, giving thanks to God the Father through him."

Colossians 3:17

"I am basically a good person. I try to do good things for other people. God knows that and will not condemn me."

A man I know, I'll call him John here, said those words to me, and I will admit, I mourned.

The thing is, John *is* a good person. He *does* do good things for other people. And God *does* know that.

But as it stands right now, he *is* condemned.

His actions will not save him when this life is over.

The reason is simple. John is not perfect. He's a good man, but he's not perfect.

And only a perfect, sinless person can stand someday in the presence of a sinless, holy, perfect God.

John cannot work his way to heaven. Neither his good intentions nor his actions will save him when he is someday judged on a standard of perfection.

But all is not lost. There is a way.

I realized this when I was 10 years old. I grew up in a Christian home with parents who had strong faith in God, and who had devoted their lives to Jesus Christ. We went to church every Sunday morning, every Sunday night, and every Wednesday night. I often saw my parents reading the Bible, and heard them talk about the importance of faithfully serving God with their lives.

I also witnessed it in their lives. They served others with no thought of reward, and were never shy about sharing their love for the Lord who had saved them. They started a church congregation in my hometown, and God blessed their efforts with spiritual and numerical growth.

I learned a lot about God, about His Son Jesus Christ, and about the Bible. I tried to live in a way that would honor God, and not displease Him, and I had actually come to believe that I was doing pretty well with that.

But I was not perfect, and in all my learning about God I came to the realization that what I was doing was not enough. My conduct and my actions could not save me.

This realization came to me in a church service, and I admit it was like a blow to the head. The preacher was talking about people who were lost, who would spend eternity after this life separated from God, because they had never acknowledged what He did for them by sending His Son to die for the forgiveness of their sins, and therefore had never surrendered their life to Him.

He was talking about people whose life had no purpose or meaning, and whose death would bring something far worse.

He was talking about me.

I actually came close to falling to my knees right there in the pew. I was so overcome with guilt for the sins I had committed against God, I could hardly contain the tears. All I wanted was to make it right, to turn everything in my life over to God, and to trust him with all my heart to save me.

I needed, and wanted, His forgiveness.

So when the preacher invited anyone who wanted to give their life to God and to accept Jesus Christ as their Lord and Savior to come forward and do it publicly, I did not hesitate. I knew that no matter what I knew, and no matter what I did, I could not save myself from being condemned at the judgment of a holy and perfect God.

I have belonged to Him ever since. Now don't get me wrong, I have been anything but perfect. In fact, at times I have been completely on the wrong path, even perhaps in defiance of Him.

But because of that decision and commitment I made at age 10, I can seek his forgiveness for my sins and receive it.

It is this commitment, this understanding of who God is and what He has done, that drives me to action.

Once you have wrapped your mind around God's grace, and given Him your heart, you will have a burning desire to serve Him, to use everything in your power to take action so that everyone you know will be saved just as you have been.

What do I mean by grace?

Have you ever read about something horrible that someone did to someone else and thought, "if that was my child, or my spouse, or my friend they did that to I would never forgive them"?

Well, every sin we commit is that horrible thing to God. Anything that violates His perfect law and perfect plan for a person's life is so awful that we cannot be near Him. He could have chosen not to forgive us, but simply to put an end to us, to end our miserable life when we sinned.

But He didn't.

When He had every right to condemn us for disobeying our Creator, He chose instead to make a way for us. Not only that, but he allowed His ungrateful creations (that would be us) to kill His only Son, His perfect Son, Jesus Christ, as a sacrifice for us so that we could live eternally in His presence.

We deserve death. He gave us life.

That's grace.

And there can be only one explanation for why He did this.

He loves us that much.

I don't know about you, but understanding God's grace and love just the little bit that I do motivates me to action. I want everyone to know who He is and what He has done.

And we are back to purpose, aren't we?

When it comes to action on God's behalf, we have to first understand that inaction is not an option. As long as we are alive on this earth, our purpose is to make known who He is and what He has done, and we cannot do that if we are doing nothing.

And the truth is, that if we are doing nothing, we have not really surrendered our life to Him, and we have not really grasped His grace, because if we had we would be completely jazzed about serving Him in some way.

I should point out here that simply attending a church service, even if it is every Sunday, is not action. It's simply what we all must do to remain strong and faithful.

Secondly, we have to also understand that there is such a thing as misguided action. This would be an action that God did not intend for us to do, and probably one that God did not gift us with the skill or talent to do.

If our heart is in it, however, if we are doing it out of pure love and thankfulness, God will often use it for His glory anyway, usually in some way that we never imagined, and maybe never even understand. We serve a limitlessly creative God.

And for Him, it's all about why we do it. He knows our hearts and our motivation, and He will use our worst efforts, our most misguided actions, in amazing ways, both for our encouragement and His glory.

Sometimes He will divert us to another action, just like any good parent will do with their child. Though we may be well-intentioned, He will direct our efforts in the way He has planned for us.

Third, we must understand that sometimes the action that God wishes us to take does not feel much like action to us. It may seem too quiet or mundane, not very exciting and maybe not even noticed by anyone.

Sometimes this is because we must learn that this kind of humble service is what God loves the most. We serve Him in complete anonymity simply because we love Him, and we demonstrate faithfulness when no one but God is looking.

Sometimes, too, it is to prepare us for the greater action that is to come. Perhaps God simply wants you to study His Word, pray, attend classes, and hear sermons for a while so that you will be positioned for your next assignment from Him. The better you know Him, and the closer you are to Him on a personal basis, the more you will be able to contribute to His kingdom.

Finally, you must come to an understanding not only that God has specific things that He wishes you to do, but also you must discover how He communicates that to you.

If you are like me, you need God to make it pretty obvious. He, of course, knows this about me, and makes it very clear. I need that, as I always seem to be looking somewhere else, and thinking about doing something He has no intention for me to do.

I can honestly say that in almost every way I serve God right now, I never would have imagined it, and at first really didn't want to do it. But when I realized what He wanted me to do, I did it, and He has blessed me with joy in all those ministries as a result.

This whole book-writing thing is the perfect example. I did not intend to write any books. I know I have some writing ability, but I certainly never would have felt qualified to write a book about God. It was His idea. He gave me the title, the chapter titles, the Scripture verses, the stories, the words, and most important of all, He gave me the life experiences I would need to write what He wanted me to write.

And that is exactly what I do. I write what He wants written. I sit down at this computer with an idea of what He wants me to write based on my study of His Word and what He has taught me in life, but with no specifics. I pray for His guidance and help, and I start writing. Three hours later, a chapter is written.

If it is hard for you to understand exactly what God wants you to do, talk to Him about it and He will communicate it to you in a way that you cannot misunderstand. You must however, be listening, and you must assume nothing. He will often surprise you with His choice of actions for you. You may not, at first, want to do what He has in mind for you to do.

Trust Him in this, though. You will not regret it.

Remember His grace.

There is one last thing about action that must be addressed, and that is this:

The only action that will save you is that of placing your faith and trust in Jesus Christ as your Lord and Savior, and surrendering your life to Him.

It's really more of a heart thing than an action thing, this acceptance of God's perfect plan to save you, but my point is that it is all that is required.

If you accepted Jesus as your Savior, and five minutes later were in a car accident and died, you would stand before God cleansed of all sin and welcomed into heaven. You would have possibly done nothing in your entire life to serve Him, but you would be saved.

The reason is simple: what Jesus did for you and me, the perfect sacrifice He made for us, was enough. Our efforts and our actions are not required. We can add nothing to His perfection.

We need only to trust Him for our salvation.

Whether you were baptized as a baby, whether you were "confirmed" in a church, whether you even ever *attended* church, no tradition or religious ceremony will determine your salvation. It will not be required if you have accepted God's plan, if you have trusted Jesus for eternal life.

But those things, or any other action, will not save you if you have *not* put your faith and trust in Him. You stand condemned without His sacrifice to cover your sins. Nothing you do can change that.

It's grace, you see.

So if you were thinking that it's too late in your life to try to work your way to heaven, it's not, because you don't have to.

And if you're thinking that you already have done enough to earn your way to heaven, you haven't, because you can't.

His actions made our salvation possible.

Our actions make this known. We live and we serve to honor Him.

His actions: grace.

Ours: gratitude.

Motivation for life that makes sense

# Chapter 9

# COMMITMENT

"Trust in the Lord and do good;
dwell in the land and enjoy safe pasture.
Delight yourself in the Lord
and he will give you the desires of your heart.
Commit your way to the Lord;
trust in him and he will do this:
He will make your righteousness shine like the dawn,
the justice of your cause like the noonday sun."

Psalm 37:3-6

"Therefore, if anyone is in Christ, he is a new creation;
the old has gone, the new has come!
All this is from God, who reconciled us to himself through
Christ and gave us the ministry of reconciliation:
that God was reconciling the world to himself in Christ,
not counting men's sins against them.
And he has committed to us the message of reconciliation.
We are therefore Christ's ambassadors, as though
God were making his appeal through us."

II Corinthians 5:17-20a

Sometimes when you start something, you *really* start something.

For the more than 20 years that I have been a financial advisor, I have always sent out Christmas cards to my clients. I typically spend quite a bit of time trying to find the exact right card, one that is both beautiful and that conveys the real reason why we celebrate Christmas: the arrival on earth of the Son of God.

At some point I also decided to put a small gift in the card. The gift had to meet three criteria: it had to be meaningful, it had to be inexpensive, and it had to be light in weight so that I would not have to add postage to mail it.

Now lest you're thinking I'm cheap (which I'm not) you have to realize that I knew early on that whatever I started I would have to continue, and that the few clients I had when I started would turn into hundreds at some point, and that this could turn into a huge expense if I didn't stick to my criteria for the gift.

I have to tell you, it is hard to meet those three criteria. I struggled with this every year, trying to come up with something that was tasteful and conveyed my respect and admiration for clients, but that was also lightweight and not too expensive.

I am happy to report that I no longer have that problem.

No, I didn't stop sending out Christmas cards with a gift in them.

About five years ago, I was talking about this dilemma with my wife Jackie. As usual, we couldn't think of anything.

And then she stunned with me with this idea: she asked me if my clients would like to receive a crocheted snowflake in their Christmas card.

My quick answer was "Yes!", but then I realized that although this met all the criteria perfectly, it would mean that she would have to crochet *hundreds* of individual snowflakes!

When I pointed this out to her (like she didn't realize it!) she calmly replied that she knew that it would take some time and effort, but that she was willing to do it.

I have to tell you, I was thrilled, but I was not surprised. This is exactly the type of person she is (and yes, I am very grateful to be married to her!).

So she crocheted hundreds of snowflakes, using the same pattern, and starched and pressed every one. We put them in the Christmas cards and mailed them out.

In the next two to three weeks I was inundated with phone calls, emails, and Christmas cards from clients who *loved* the snowflake. This was both good news and bad news. The good news is that it was the perfect gift, and very much appreciated. The bad news? There was no way I could equal that gift the next year.

That is when Jackie made the commitment to make a snowflake for every client every Christmas. She chooses a new pattern every year, and starts making them in January so that she can have them all made in plenty of time. It is a huge undertaking, but she takes it all in stride.

And clients who have been with me at least five years have five different hand-crocheted snowflakes. Most people have them on their Christmas tree every year. I still get calls and emails and Christmas cards expressing thanks for the snowflake every year.

I make sure they know who made them, and I always share the wonderful feedback I get with Jackie.

She made a *commitment* to make the snowflakes every year, and she has been faithful in keeping that commitment.

And we have come to the point in life where we have the desire and the willingness to make a commitment to God.

How did we get there?

We acknowledged that God is our Creator, and that He, as a result, has supremacy and authority over everything.

We came to understand that He shaped us the way He did on purpose and for a reason.

We learned that He has a direction for our life, and that He will reveal it to us.

We found out that our life has a purpose, to make known through how we live who God is and what He has done.

We discovered that a life surrendered to God has incredible meaning...every day of our life.

We realized that our best intentions are rarely carried out, but God's intention for us can be if we allow Him into our life.

We accepted the truth that others not from God will often try to distract us from His mission for our life, and that we need to stay focused on Him to stay on the path He has chosen for us.

We then knew from all this that God wants us to take action, that He has made a way for us to be saved through His grace, and that we must acknowledge and accept His free gift.

In taking that action, we surrendered everything to Him, and now we are committed to a life that is all about Him.

If we keep that commitment, our life will always have purpose and meaning, and we will always have hope and peace, no matter what difficulties we face.

And still we have trouble with commitments, don't we?

The two times each year when people make the most commitments are New Year's and Lent. There are the inevitable New Year's resolutions, which are rarely kept, even though they are commitments.

People usually "give up something" for Lent, and I really do think most people keep these commitments *during* Lent, but then go back to partaking in whatever they gave up for Lent when it's over.

The very meaning of the word commitment has been compromised in our society. Though commitment implies an ongoing and never-ending pledge, in our world today it seems it can be terminated if it lasts even a short time.

How many athletes or coaches can you think of who sign a contract they will probably never see all the way through?

How many people stating wedding vows are really making a commitment for the rest of their life?

How many people running for political office actually keep the commitments they made in the campaign once they are elected?

How many times has someone used the word "promise" with you and not come through as promised?

More importantly, how often have you made commitments that, despite your best intentions at the time of the commitment, you did not keep?

If you think about it, you will realize that commitments are about *others*. When we break our commitments, it is because we have lost our focus on others, and started focusing only on ourselves. Though we would "like to keep our commitment", we "have to think of our own self-interest".

The most incredible and wonderful thing about a commitment to God is that He will help us do what our human nature will not seem to let us do. He will help us to focus our life on Him, and on the needs of other people.

The reason we can do this is because He has our life in His hands, and we can be totally reliant on Him for everything we might need. We do not need to worry or think about ourselves at all. He has that under control.

We have surrendered that control to Him, and because He is perfectly faithful, we do not need to focus on our own will at all.

Not that we don't, mind you. Sometimes we allow ourselves to feel sorry for ourselves, or worry about our needs, or commiserate over some injustice that has been done to us.

But if we have made a commitment to live our life the way God wants us to live it, there are some things we can do to access His power to overcome our weaknesses and the temptation to back off that commitment.

The first is to pray. Talk to God. He is the greatest friend we could ever have, and He is a great listener. Tell Him that despite your desire to serve Him and be true to Him, you are struggling with concerns. Ask Him to help you to remain faithful. Thank Him for His love and grace, and the blessings He has given you.

Be real with Him. Talk as you would talk to someone who you totally trust. Tell Him everything. Let your emotion out. Cry if you need to. If you blubber or mumble or say it wrong He will still understand. Remember He loves you.

The second way is to read His words. Read the Bible. These are the very words of the One who created you. He speaks to you in this way, and you will be amazed by the power in His words.

In the Bible you will read His promises. He keeps them all forever.

You will find encouragement. There are others who have had bad things happen to them too, many much worse than what you are going through. Read what He did for them, and know that He will be there for you, too. There are others who have had doubts and fears and temptations. Read what He did to lift them up and strengthen them when they had no place to turn and were feeling powerless, and know that He will do the same for you.

You will find instruction. There is a way He desires for you to live in order to keep your commitment to Him. If you live this way, it will give your life meaning, and you will never wonder what your purpose is.

The Bible is so amazingly relevant to your life today. The words will constantly remind you of who God is, what He has done, and what it all means in the context of what you will be doing today. As you get to know Him better, you will find Him directing you right into His will, and strengthening you in your commitment to Him.

The third way to keep our commitment to God is accountability. We need to involve other people who love Him as we do, and who have made the same commitment, in our effort to keep ours.

We do not like this way very much. Admitting our failures to God in private is one thing, but talking about them openly with another person is quite another.

But there are three things about accountability that make it very effective, and a lot more appealing than we may first think.

The first is that we are not *always* sharing our failures and our fears. We are also sharing our joys and successes. We are sharing the little doses of grace that God gives us when we are faithful, and thus we are encouraging this person to keep their commitment as well.

The second is that the person to whom we have made ourselves accountable is just as we are: very human, sometimes weak, at times struggling, always striving but not always succeeding. We can be as much of a help to them as they are to us.

The third is that God puts people in our lives for a reason. We need them, and He knows that. He also knows that these relationships are a source of joy for us, knowing that we are not alone in this world, and that our love for and commitment to God is something we share with other people.

Accountability is most effectively established through a great church, and at a number of different levels. It is certainly the easiest to access this way. However, God will often, as we search for the right church, put a person or two in our life that will help us to grow and stay faithful in our commitment.

We all admire people who keep their commitments, but for me the one person I admire the most for this is my mother.

My mom has always been a woman who kept her commitments...to everyone in her life and to God. That is an amazing thing to say about anyone, but especially about someone who is nearly 80 years old.

I especially remember the way she cared for my grandmother. My grandmother's health deteriorated, and Mom cared for her in my grandma's home as long as she could. When that was no longer possible, she visited her in the nursing home every day.

What makes that especially remarkable is that my grandmother, who had suffered a series of small strokes, was really quite cruel to my mother. She never seemed to do anything quite right in my grandmother's eyes, and took a lot of verbal abuse over the years Grandma was at home with her as well as in the nursing home.

But it did not deter Mom in her commitment. She was faithful to her mother, and in the process faithful to her God to the very end of Grandma's life.

For Mom this faithfulness always came back to the same thing: God always has been and always will be faithful in His commitment to her. He sent His Son to die so that He might save her. He wanted her to honor her mother.

Enough said. Case closed. Commitment made and kept.

And so it is for each of us. The One who created you, and who you sinned against, made a commitment to save you because He loves you.

The very least we can do is to make a commitment to Him... and keep it.

# Chapter 10

# TIME

"There is a time for everything, and a season for every
activity under heaven:
a time to be born and a time to die,
a time to plant and time to uproot,
a time to kill and a time to heal,
a time to tear down and a time to build,
a time to weep and a time to laugh,
a time to mourn and a time to dance,
a time to scatter stones and a time to gather them,
a time to embrace and a time to refrain,
a time to search and a time to give up,
a time to keep and a time to throw away,
a time to tear and a time to mend,
a time to be silent and a time to speak,
a time to love and a time to hate,
a time for war and a time for peace."

Ecclesiastes 3:1-8


"Be very careful, then, how you live - not as unwise but as
wise, making the most of every opportunity, because the
days are evil."

Ephesians 5:15-16

Let me tell you about two people I know.

You know them too, although the people you know are not the same as the ones I know.

Confused? Probably.

But my point is that we all know two people like these two.

The first, I'll call him Sam, is, to put it mildly, an inefficient disaster.

Sam starts many things, and finishes almost none of them.

Sam can spend a lot of time on something meaningless, and put off something important. However, he still doesn't finish the unimportant thing he's working on.

Sam, in the middle of doing something he needs to do, thinks of something he should do or would rather do and starts doing that.

Sam plans to do a lot of things, although he rarely makes a list of them, so he forgets most of them. If he does make a list, he loses it or never looks at it.

Sam is late for pretty much everything he attends, if he remembers to attend at all.

Sam eats when he is hungry and sleeps when he is tired, no matter what time of day or night it is.

Sam's house, office desk, and hobby area are a mess, unless he has someone in his life who picks up after him.

Sam does a lot of things at the last minute, pushing deadlines to their limits. He is in the line at the post office mailing his taxes on the evening of April 15.

I like comparing myself to Sam.

The second person, I'll call her Sarah (this is not a reflection on men and women), is a marvel of organization and efficiency.

Sarah starts many things, and finishes all of them, sometimes one at a time and sometimes several at the same time.

Sarah prioritizes things she needs to do and completes them in the order of their importance, and even delegates unimportant things to others.

Sarah is rarely distracted from the task at hand, but if she is she quickly returns to it and completes it.

Sarah plans to do a lot of things, and is involved in a lot of things. She often makes a list so she won't forget anything and follows it precisely.

Sarah never forgets to attend something she intended or promised to attend, and always arrives early.

Sarah eats at regular times each day, and goes to bed and rises at the same time each day. She even knows how much sleep she needs to be at her best.

Sarah's house, office desk, and hobby area are always neat and tidy, unless she has someone in her life who makes a mess of them at times.

Sarah never misses a deadline, and is usually done long before something is due. She usually does her taxes the first week of February and files online to get her refund quickly.

I do *not* enjoy comparing myself to Sarah. I do marvel at her, however.

As you were reading this, you no doubt thought of the names of the two people in your life who are like these two.

Odds are one of the names was not your own. You are probably somewhere in between the two.

If you narrow it down to the biggest difference between the two, you would have to say that it is how they use their time.

Time is a gift from God. God gives us many great gifts, but time is one of the greatest. And like so many of the gifts He gives us, He allows us the freedom to use it as we choose. It seems that if we use it wisely and for His glory, He perhaps will give us more.

Or perhaps He will give us less.

It kind of depends on your perspective, doesn't it?

Time is a limited resource. We only have so much of it.

The thing is, we don't know how much we are going to get, so it is important to make the most of it.

To some people this means living every day like it's your last day on earth, pursuing whatever pleasures there are out there, seeking to find happiness in anything and everything.

But to the person who knows their Creator, almighty God, and who has granted him the authority in their life, it means both the same thing and something different.

It means you live every day like it's your last day on earth (the same), pursuing the path God has laid out for you and seeking to make known who God is and what He has done (different).

It means you don't have to pursue anything but a stronger relationship with God, and the joy and peace will come from Him.

I have been teaching 3$^{rd}$ grade Sunday School for nearly 11 years, and for the last eight years have used the same curriculum. In the course of a year, we cover the life of Jesus while He was here on earth. Every week and every year I learn more about Him.

One of the things I have learned from Jesus is how I should spend my time. He was the perfect model of using every moment He was given on earth to glorify God, and to make known who God is and how He wants us to live.

Jesus *represented* His Father, God, in every moment of His life on earth.

And that should be our goal.

So if you want to learn from the perfect Master, read the books of Matthew, Mark, Luke and John in the Bible and look carefully at how Jesus spent His time.

Now I know that we fall short of that, but rather than throw in the towel in defeat we need to examine what we do with our time and be honest about what we do that is honoring God and what is not.

The simple parts are on the extremes. There are some things we do that are just the opposite of God-honoring, things we would not want to be doing when Jesus returns. These things we have to eliminate, and if our desire is to do that and we ask God to help us and forgive us, He absolutely will.

There is *nothing* beyond His power.

Remember that.

On the other extreme are the things we do that are absolutely God-honoring. When we pray to Him, when we read His Bible, or when we are involved in some area of ministry or service to Him, clearly this is time well spent.

On both extremes the time we spend is optional. But what about the time we spend that is not optional?

There are things we spend time on that we *have* to do. They are not optional.

We have to go to work or to school. We have to go to the grocery store and buy food. We have to go to the doctor. We have to spend time mowing the lawn or cleaning the house.

Aren't these time-wasters? Is there any way we can honor God when we are doing these required and necessary things?

I'm glad you asked...there is!

In Colossians 3:23-24 we read these amazing and encouraging words: "Whatever you do, work at it with all your heart, as working for the Lord, not for men, since you know that you will receive an inheritance from the Lord as a reward. It is the Lord Christ you are serving."

It is all about our attitude, and how we can make the time we spend doing these things meaningful to God. We can choose to work hard at these things, as if they are the same kind of Lord's work as teaching a Sunday School class, or we can do the minimum necessary to get by.

Are we kind to everyone in the workplace, or in school? Or are there people we are not kind to because they rub us the wrong way? Are we cranky or moody? Do people avoid us because we are hard to get along with or hard to predict? Or are we always reflecting the example Jesus set for us? Are we always doing more than asked, or do others see us try to skate by without doing too much?

God has us in these places for a reason, part of His plan for our life. It is for both our benefit and the benefit of others for us to spend this necessary and required time in a place where what we do and say is always on display.

Even the necessary things we do with our time that require us to be alone are important. I get some of my best thinking done while I am riding the lawn tractor. I can reflect on Bible verses I read that morning, or look around as I ride and thank God for the beauty of His creation, or I can thank Him for the house and yard He has provided. I often find myself singing songs of praise to God, which is especially nice since the lawn tractor is loud and no one can hear me (you know, in case I'm not really in tune!).

Yes, there is much we can do to honor God with the time we spend doing the necessary things in life.

And then there are the optional times, the times we can do what we choose. This is where self-reflection and examination are especially important, and, I must admit, particularly difficult.

Much of what we do during this time develops a pattern, and we tend to get into this pattern and follow it on a regular basis. We do certain things at certain times of day or on certain days, and although we do have control of these things they can and do take on a life of their own. After a while we do them automatically.

We all need to look at these activities carefully. Most of them aren't bad or good, but they are most definitely honoring to God or they are not, depending on how and why we do them. To change these "habits" requires a concerted effort and quite a bit of time. It is said that to establish something new in your life as a regular habit (such as Bible reading, for example) requires doing it for 21 consecutive days.

I have several activities that I do to unwind and to relax. One of them is to play a game called Free Cell, which I'm sure most of you have heard of or seen. I have become so good at this game I can play it totally without thinking. But I have discovered that my mind is free to think about things that I have been reading or studying, or about what things I need to continue or change in my life. I also often think about my spiritual goals while I am playing this game. Interestingly, I now find that my mind automatically goes to these things whenever I play it. It's like I associate playing the game with thinking about important things.

A second thing I like to do is put together jigsaw puzzles. In our home there is almost always a jigsaw puzzle set up in the living room. This not only allows me to slow down and relax, but it keeps me from watching mindless shows on television, which I have been known to do, and which usually has no merit whatsoever.

Often, too, when I work on the puzzle with my wife Jackie or my daughter Jasmine we get the chance to talk, something at which we could all spend more time.

You can take your own optional activities and evaluate them as time-wasters or as valuable in your relationship with God, not necessarily because of what you are doing, but because God is or is not in the front of your mind when you are doing them.

The final key in making the most of the time God has given you involves an understanding that you must make a proactive choice to use it wisely.

This is the test that must be put to any use of your time. It is also the test that must be put to your attitude regarding any activity.

It should be a matter of daily prayer that God would grant us the wisdom to make the choices with our time that would most honor Him.

It is this wisdom and this preparation that makes it possible for us to see and take advantage of every opportunity to make Him known to other people.

And that is what He wants us to do with the time He has given us.

Although you know a Sam, and you know a Sarah, you are probably not like either one of them.

Nor do you want to be.

You want to be like Jesus.

Your time is precious and limited.

Go make Him known.

# Chapter 11

# PERSEVERANCE

"Therefore, since we have been justified through faith, we have peace with God through our Lord Jesus Christ, through whom we have gained access by faith into this grace in which we now stand. And we rejoice in the hope of the glory of God. Not only so, but we also rejoice in our sufferings, because we know that suffering produces perseverance; perseverance, character; and character, hope. And hope does not disappoint us, because God has poured out his love into our hearts by the Holy Spirit, whom he has given us."

Romans 5:1-5

"Consider it pure joy, my brothers, whenever you face trials of many kinds, because you know that the testing of your faith develops perseverance.
Perseverance must finish its work so that you may be mature and complete, not lacking anything. If any of you lacks wisdom, he should ask God, who gives generously to all without finding fault, and it will be given to him."

James 1:2-5

"You need to persevere so that when you have done the will of God, you will receive what he has promised."

Hebrews 10:36

"Be faithful, even to the point of death, and I will give you the crown of life."

Revelation 2:10b

It was one of the most surprising phone calls I have ever received.

One of those "doses of grace". But a *big* dose.

This client of mine, I'll call him Joe, called me at the office one day. Joe and his wife, I'll call her Terry, had been clients of mine for quite some time, but were inconsistent about coming in for appointments, and our conversations never went much past financial plans and investment strategies, although not for lack of effort on my part.

I have always believed that the better I get to know a client, the more I will be able to help them achieve their goals. I have also always known that faith in the God that both created them and entrusted them with money will lead them to making sound decisions and free their life from worry.

But it had honestly been a bit difficult to get to know them. They were pretty quiet about their personal and family life.

Which made the phone call from Joe all the more surprising.

"This may be the strangest phone call you ever received," is the way Joe started.

But then he said the words that thrilled my heart.

"I want to talk to you about Jesus Christ."

Well, though I was happy to do that with Joe, and I told him so, I was more than a little curious about where this phone call was coming from, so I simply asked him the question.

"What is going on in your life, Joe?"

Joe proceeded to tell me that about six months ago he had been arrested for drunken driving...for the *second* time. And now he was going to have to spend some time in jail.

After the arrest, he began to understand his problem ran deeper than drinking. He understood that he was filling a big void in his life with alcohol, and that alcohol was not going to get it done. He thought maybe the answer was God.

I don't really know why he came to that conclusion, but I do know that God planted it in some way because He loves Joe so much. It may have been the church he went to as a child, and which he had long since abandoned. It may have been people that God put in Joe's life to point him toward his Creator.

So, Joe told me, he began to seek God.

And you know what God promised: if you seek Him, you *will* find Him.

Joe returned to church, and he began to get involved. He read and studied his Bible intensely. And he prayed. He prayed a lot, and about everything.

Eventually one of those prayers was a prayer of commitment of his life to Jesus Christ, because he realized it was the only way he could truly be saved from his empty and lost condition.

He began to openly communicate all of this to Terry and to their three children. It was pretty confusing to them at first, but they clearly began to like the changes they were seeing in him.

And now he had to pay the penalty for his past foolishness, and he was overwhelmed with dread. He could go to work during the day, but had to sit in jail from the time he got off work until he went back to work the next morning.

"How am I ever going to get through this?" he asked me. "How can Jesus help me get through this?"

We talked about practical things at first. Spending the time reading his Bible as well as books that will build his faith would be a great idea. I gave him some book titles that would help him grow in his walk with God. We tossed around the idea of keeping a journal of his experience that could be shared with others at some point later on.

But when we got right down to it, the way he was going to persevere was to spend his time meditating and praying, demonstrating his ever-increasing love for Jesus and his continual desire to know Jesus better, thus building his faith into a power beyond his own ability, a power granted by Almighty God.

After all, Jesus was the one who persevered through a lot more than jail. He endured a painful and unjust death on a cross because this was God's plan to save people like Joe.

And like you and me.

Joe got through the jail experience, and because of his faithfulness God was able to use that time to build his faith and his character. Joe and his family do nothing now without trying to determine if it is God's will, and God has truly blessed them for their devotion to Him.

The subject of perseverance is not an easy one, because to have perseverance means to have hardship.

Perseverance is not persistence. You can be persistent without having anything difficult going on in your life. You need perseverance when you are suffering.

And make no mistake about it, you *are* going to have some very difficult times in your life, and you are going to be free to decide how you are going to endure them.

God's definition of perseverance is more than just simple endurance. It is enduring *and* remaining faithful to Him through it all.

And He knows you can do it, because He will help you if your heart is turned toward Him. He has promised this, and He keeps His promises.

To prove it He has given us many, many examples of this in the Bible. If you read Hebrews 11, you will see that time after time when a person who loves God is in the middle of even a frightening hardship, God will see them through. Their faith actually builds through the hardship, because God continually demonstrates His love for them and empowers them beyond their own ability.

After all the examples in Hebrews 11, it says this in Hebrews 12:1-3:

"Therefore, since we are surrounded by such a great cloud of witnesses, let us throw off everything that hinders and the sin that so easily entangles, and let us run with perseverance the race marked out for us. Let us fix our eyes on Jesus, the author and perfecter of our faith, who for the joy set before him endured the cross, scorning its shame, and sat down at the right hand of the throne of God. Consider him who endured such opposition from sinful men, so that you will not grow weary and lose heart."

Notice the words "consider him".

You see, it all comes down to who you worship.

Now it is important at this point to understand what it means to worship, because the real meaning of the word has been tainted and diminished in our world.

Think about it. If a young boy worships a professional athlete, he doesn't worship him one day a week for an hour. He doesn't just sing songs about him once in a while. He admires and looks up to this athlete all the time.

If a young man worships a young woman, he doesn't spend one hour a week with her, adorning her with praise for that one hour, then ignore her the rest of the week. He loves and adores her 24/7.

So it is if you worship Jesus Christ. To worship Him means to make Him the center of your life, to love and admire and adore and look up to Him every moment of every day. It means to be like Him in every way possible.

You cannot worship Him in a church service one hour a week. If you truly worship Him, it will define who you are.

That's what "fix our eyes on Jesus" means.

And why should we do this? Should we do this so that when trouble comes, He will helps us persevere?

No, we should do this, and will do this, because we have "considered" Him.

There has never been a greater act of love, or a greater injustice, than Jesus dying on the cross. He came down from the glory of heaven to this place where all these selfish and sinful people are, and He lived a perfect life in total obedience to God, and then He allowed these same people He came to save to kill Him without cause.

If you "consider" what He did for you, how could you not worship Him? How could you ever take your eyes off One like that?

Could you stay faithful to a God like that through whatever hardship comes?

I know I can.

And as if that wasn't enough, God raised Jesus from the dead, and Jesus now sits at the right hand of God, waiting for the word from God so He can come back and gather up those who have been faithful, who have persevered, to come be with Him forever.

And as if *that* wasn't enough, God sent His own Holy Spirit to comfort us, to counsel us, to teach us, and to strengthen us with His power when we are in the middle of those times when we need to persevere.

Probably the greatest example in history of faithful perseverance was Job. Here was a man of great wealth and influence, a man with everything most people would ever want in life, and yet a man who was faithful to God in the midst of all this blessing.

Job lost everything. He lost his family, every possession he had, and his health.

Job knew who God was. He knew God was not paying him back for some sin he had committed. He knew God was aware of what was happening. He knew God had some plans and did some things he was not able to understand. He praised the name of God in the middle of the worst hardship any man has ever had.

At one point he wavered just a little and asked God to explain what was going on. To us this is understandable. Anyone would, after all, want to understand why he had to go through something like this. We've all been there.

The last five chapters of the book of Job are a must-read if you're trying to persevere through a tough time. God in these chapters reminds Job of who He (God) is, what He has done, and what He can do. He asks Job whether he (Job) can do any of these things.

It is truly an amazing list.

Job is deeply humbled by God's answer. He is humbled not only by what God said, but that God would even answer him, a simple man with no understanding of the great things of God.

God in those chapters answers the "Why me, God?" question for all of us for all time. We can persevere because He is in control, because He has a greater plan than we can ever understand, because He loves us, and because He will never forsake us.

He will see us through it.

You and I have seen it, haven't we? The examples are not just in the Bible. We know people who have gone through incredibly difficult times, and who have never wavered in their trust in the God who is supreme in the universe.

And He has stood by them.

I know, because I am one of those people. And I am profoundly grateful that He didn't put me through it until my faith was strong enough to withstand the test.

But you will get that story later in the book.

Maybe you have some difficulty in your life right now. Lots of people do.

Maybe it's a financial problem, and you can't see how it could possibly be resolved.

Maybe it's a relationship issue, and your heart is breaking as it all seems to be falling apart.

Maybe you're grieving the loss of a loved one, and it seems like you'll never shake the sadness and pain you feel.

Maybe it's a health issue, and you feel that you will never be whole again.

Maybe it's a feeling of emptiness, and you've tried to fill it with drugs, or alcohol, or other people, or a job, and it's just not working.

I'm here to tell you that you *can* persevere.

You can get through this.

Consider Him who endured the cross...for you.

Fix your eyes on Jesus.

# Chapter 12

# GOAL

"However, I consider my life worth nothing to me, if only I may finish the race and complete the task the Lord Jesus has given me - the task of testifying to the gospel of God's grace."

Acts 20:24

"Do you not know that in a race all the runners run, but only one gets the prize?
Run in such a way as to get the prize. Everyone who competes in the games goes into strict training. They do it to get a crown that will not last; but we do it to get a crown that will last forever."

I Corinthians 9:24-25

"Not that I have already obtained all this, or have already been made perfect, but I press on to take hold of that for which Christ Jesus took hold of me. Brothers, I do not consider myself yet to have taken hold of it. But one thing I do:

Forgetting what is behind and straining toward what is ahead, I press on toward the goal to win the prize for which God has called me heavenward in Christ Jesus."

Philippians 3:12-14

"Therefore we are always confident and know that as long as we are at home in the body we are away from the Lord. We live by faith, not by sight. We are confident, I say, and would prefer to be away from the body and at home with the Lord. So we make it our goal to please him, whether we are at home in the body or away from it. For we must all appear before the judgment seat of Christ, that each one may receive what is due him for the things done while in the body, whether good or bad."

II Corinthians 5:6-10

It has been nearly 50 years since I last saw him, and yet I will never forget him.

His name was Bill Beadle.

Funny name, huh? And nobody made more jokes about his name than Bill Beadle himself.

But it was not his name that caused me to remember him so well. It was the man.

In my entire life I have never met anyone with a better understanding of what God did to save him.

And with that incredible knowledge and wisdom came his life goal: to tell everyone he could possibly tell as long as he had breath.

Bill Beadle was a retired farmer, and I'm guessing he was in his 70's when I met him.

But retirement to Bill meant simply that he could spend more time telling people about God's amazing gift of grace.

He wrote a book about it, and according to him he wrote the book so that he would not forget one single detail, and so that people would have something to refer to and study long after he had left their town. I still have an old, dog-eared copy of that book...little did Bill know that I would have something to refer to and study decades after he went home to be with his beloved Lord.

Because you see, Bill Beadle went from farming to evangelism. He went from place to place preaching the gospel, anywhere and everywhere people would invite him. He came to our city for a week at a time, and spoke every night of that week in our church. His sermons were more like lessons, and he used visual aids like charts and graphs to help us to understand what he had found in the Bible.

But it was his energy and enthusiasm that really captured you. He was so *excited* about God's gift of salvation, and so obviously driven to tell everyone he could so that they, too, would be saved, and would spend eternity (with him) in heaven. He would literally motivate you to want to go to heaven because *he* would be there!

Bill referred to his wife as "Mama", a name that I suppose would make him quite politically incorrect these days. But he spoke that name with such love and respect, you knew it was the most endearing name he could think of. If I ever knew Mrs. Beadle's first name, I don't remember it. I do remember "Mama" quite well.

The Beadle's stayed in our home when they were in our city, and I thank God often to this day for that blessing. Bill often sat and talked with me, and I also sat in and listened when he and my dad were talking.

So I know this, though it was maybe years later before it became a conscious thought:

Bill Beadle's life was defined by his goal. And his goal was to serve and honor and please his Lord and Savior, Jesus Christ.

Because he understood so well that Jesus, by God's grace, had saved him from being eternally condemned.

You could not talk to Bill Beadle for five minutes without understanding that his life was not about him...it was about God.

And ever since I met the man, I have wanted that to be me. Though it has certainly not always been, I have tried to strive in that direction, hoping that someday people would look at me and define me by the God I love.

We all have goals. Some of them are very short-term goals. It might be our goal to get through the day. It might be our goal to get a project at work or school or home done. It might be our goal to read a book, or write a letter, or to finish all the things on the list we made of things we had to do. We might have a goal that requires a few days, or a few weeks, or a few months.

Created by God the way we are, we need a mission. We need something to strive for, to reach for, so that when we accomplish it we will have this great sense of satisfaction. We need to experience growth in our life, and as importantly, we need to see that growth ourselves.

We have a group that meets in our home we call a Care Group. We meet every two weeks, and have for over 10 years. It is a diverse group, made up of men and women, singles and couples, young and old.

Despite this diversity, we have one purpose in meeting: to grow in our relationship with God.

We always have a book we are reading and studying that addresses how we can grow spiritually. We discuss a chapter in the book, and look at Bible passages that direct us in this particular area. We spend time talking about what people or situations are in need of prayer, and we pray. At the end of the evening we simply fellowship with each other, sharing a snack and conversation.

An atmosphere of tremendous trust exists in this group, and that trust translates into encouragement, help and strength in each one of us.

A few years ago we started setting personal goals, and sharing the goals with each other. We did it at my insistence, and admittedly some have embraced the idea more than others, but the ones who have seem to have grown the most.

You see, I observed that nearly all of these people were growing rather dramatically in their personal relationship with God, but they did not know it. God was prodding them forward, and they were responding, but it struck me that they did not see how much they were growing spiritually. Thus they were not experiencing the joy and motivation they might have if they could see what I could see.

So we now set spiritual goals every six months. There's nothing magical about that time period, but if the time period is too short, the goals tend to be too easy or too hard, and if the time period is too long it is too difficult to sustain. Every six months each person talks about their progress the past six months, and their goal for the next six months.

There is a direct correlation between the commitment to the goal and the personal spiritual growth a person experiences.

If a person is not committed to the goal, there will be little growth and little joy as a result. If one grudgingly makes a goal, and gives little thought or prayer to what God would want that goal to be, they will progress little, and will, in fact, have trouble staying focused on the goal.

If a person is committed to the goal, and makes that goal after much meditation and prayer, God will bless them in ways beyond their imagination.

Since I was the one that initiated goals in our Care Group, I obviously believe they are important, and I have given it high priority in my own life. I am also blessed to have a great friend as an accountability partner to keep me focused on my goal, not to mention encouraged, as I pursue a stronger relationship with God.

The goal I set every six months generally has to do with some area of my life in which God has revealed to me that I need to work on. For example, one of my goals a year or so ago was to become better at letting God do His work in other people's lives, and to be silent when God wants me to be silent. Often I talk too much, and try to fix things in other people's lives when what they need is to turn to God.

Toward that end I studied many of God's amazing acts of grace in people's lives throughout history, both in my Bible and in other people's books. I prayed about it daily, and it helped me to be more aware. God helped me to think before I spoke, and sometimes to not speak at all.

In the process of growing in this area, I developed a pattern in my life that I was able to continue beyond the six months, and God has blessed me with more discernment in this area because I sought His help.

But all of this is still about shorter-term goals, and what we really want in life is a big-picture goal. We want something to pursue for our entire lifetime.

Which brings me back to Bill Beadle, whose life was defined by his goal.

And it was clear to everyone who met him what his goal was: to serve and honor and please his Lord and Savior, Jesus Christ. Everyone, including Bill himself, defined him as a man who loved Jesus.

How would people define you? How would you define yourself?

Try this experiment. Think of someone you especially like. Describe them in one word or short phrase.

I tried this in a small sample group of people, and I heard words and phrases like "kind", "a great listener", "compassionate", "caring", "joyful", "a great friend", "wise", "happy", and even one "honors God with his life".

You may have come up with different words or phrases, but wouldn't you love to be defined with any of these?

Could you be?

Now think of someone you don't especially like. Describe *them* in one word or short phrase.

I tried this one on my sample group, as well. I heard words and phrases like "cruel", "selfish", "controlling", "cold", "grumpy", "unpleasant", "no fun to be around", "self-centered", "annoying", "pushy", and even one "nasty".

Again, you may have come up with different words or phrases, but wouldn't it grieve you to be defined this way by other people?

Could you be?

Now comes the hard part. If you look at yourself very honestly, what word or phrase defines you?

And if that word or phrase you came up with defines you, what does that say about your life goal?

One more question: would other people define you the same way you did, or would they have a different word or phrase?

The point is we will live our life based on our goal, and that goal will define us, to ourselves and to others.

God gives us a goal. It is to live a life that pleases Him. We will never totally achieve this goal, but it is the devotion to this goal, and the journey toward it, that He blesses so totally and overwhelmingly.

The peace and joy that you experience with a life goal of pleasing God cannot be achieved any other way.

God created you and shaped you for this. He directs you, and gives your life meaning and purpose, for this.

Bill Beadle never accomplished his goal. I'm sure he accomplished more than he ever dreamed because of the way God blessed what he did and said. I'm pretty sure he is and will continue to be amazed at all the people in heaven because of his life goal.

Bill knew, though, that his goal would never be completely accomplished. He just had such joy because his journey through life while striving for his goal was so incredibly satisfying. God blessed his efforts, and empowered him beyond his human capability, because Bill defined himself as a disciple of Jesus Christ.

He wanted to be as much like Jesus as he possibly could.

In my opinion, he got very, very close to his goal.

He was this way because he understood that as a sinner he had no way to save himself. He understood that he could never leave this earth and stand before a perfect and holy God and defend the sinful actions and attitudes in his life. He understood that Jesus, the perfect Son of God, had given His life so that he could spend eternity with his Creator. He understood that he, Bill Beadle, had done nothing to deserve this.

He understood it was God's grace.

He was defined by this, and his life goal was to live to honor the One who did this for him. He kept this in the front of his mind until the day he left this earth to be with the One who meant everything to him.

Everything.

It is my prayer that someday someone could write a chapter like this about you, that you would be defined as a man or woman who above all lived to serve and honor and please your Lord and Savior, Jesus Christ.

Because, you see, whether you ever accept Him as your Lord and Savior or not, He still died to save you.

And if you do accept Him, your life, defined by your love for Him, will make sense.

## Part II

# DEATH

# Chapter 13

# INEVITABILITY

"Like water spilled on the ground, which cannot be recovered, so we must die.
But God does not take away life; instead, he devises ways so that a banished person may not remain estranged from him."

II Samuel 14:14

"For all can see that wise men die; the foolish and the senseless alike perish and leave their wealth to others. Their tombs will remain their houses forever, their dwellings for endless generations, though they had named lands after themselves. But man, despite his riches, does not endure; he is like the beasts that perish."

Psalm 49:10-12

"Therefore, just as sin entered the world through one man, and death through sin, and in this way death came to all men, because all sinned...."

Romans 5:12

I t is a phrase I have heard hundreds of times.
"If something happens to me...."

In my work, in the world of financial planning, we plan for everything. Probably everyone's least favorite is to plan for the event of what is termed "untimely death". What that term means is not that death is unexpected, or that death is possibly not going to happen, but it means a death that comes earlier than most people.

We look at that possibility, because it could happen, and we examine whether someone left behind would be financially vulnerable and therefore needs to be protected. Often the solution is life insurance, money paid to a survivor at death. Pure and simple, this is a calculated risk a life insurance company takes, a bet they are making that the person will live a long time. They make this bet after a careful examination of the person, trying to determine if there is any reason to believe this person might not live a good long time.

My financial planning software does not use the term "death", nor does it use the words "John dies" in the module that calculates whether these people need any life insurance. Instead it uses the term "Mary survives" to indicate that John has died.

To be perfectly honest, I find this somewhat amusing. Apparently the word "death" is too insensitive or harsh. Yet by using the term "Mary survives" you have to actually think about it and realize that this means John died. In other words, you simply cannot escape this reality.

It's not a question of *whether* John will die, it's simply a question of *when*.

We are all terminal.

We are all going to die.

Most people do not like to think about this, which is why I said it is everyone's least favorite financial planning topic.

I find this interesting, and when I get the chance, I always explore why death is something they don't wish to think about or talk about any more than necessary.

For some people, they put themselves in the place of those they love who are left behind after they die, and imagine the grief and difficulty those loved ones will have to deal with. They think about their wife or husband or children in particular, and wish to live so that these people will not have to suffer the loss.

For other people, they don't fear death, they fear the dying. They don't want to suffer prolonged pain in the process. They know what will happen after they die, but *how* they might die makes them prefer not to think about it.

But for most people, they don't like to think about death because they fear what comes next. It is, to most people, an unknown, and they are not ready to face that unknown. It will be out of their hands, and they will be powerless, and that is not a good thought for a lot of people.

Regardless where you fall in those three groups, it is still inevitable that you are someday going to die. We can use other words, like "leave this earth" or "pass away", which sound a little better, but it doesn't change a thing.

We live in a world which is fond of compromising truth. People have found that by using different words, they can make sinful acts appear not so bad, maybe even acceptable. Apparently the theory is that if you repeat a lie often enough and to enough people, it will be accepted as truth.

But you can't do that with death. It is inevitable.

In fact, articles could appear in the newspaper and on the internet, and government leaders could give speeches, and ads could be endlessly run on television during the most popular shows, and sports stars and famous actors could give interviews, all saying that we will all live forever and no one will die, and still, one after the other, people will die.

We could market the whole "No More Death" campaign using every resource we have, and still people would not believe it.

Because we know...we are all going to die.

And here is the real question about that:

Why?

The answer to that question goes all the way back to Adam and Eve.

God created Adam, and from Adam's rib created Eve, and those two had the perfect life. Why, God had even created them "in His own image"!

They had this perfect relationship with God. They had plenty of food. They had a wonderful place to live. They had absolute safety and security. They had need of nothing.

And they only had one rule: do not eat the fruit of the tree of knowledge of good and evil.

Just that one rule.

It was not in their best interests to upset their perfect life by having knowledge of good and evil, so God told them to stay away from that tree.

We know what happened next don't we? Eve was tempted by the serpent, who told her she would be equal to God if she ate that fruit, and once she gave in and ate it, she wanted Adam to eat it too so she wouldn't be alone in her guilt.

And of course he did eat it, and then the two of them were miserable together in their guilt for violating the one rule God gave them.

And now everything had changed. The relationship, so perfect before, was now less than perfect because they had damaged it.

The worst part was, they knew it. And they had to live with it.

The Bible says in Romans 6:23 "the wages of sin is death".

That is God's punishment for disobedience. It was then and it is now. You may have heard something different than that, but God does not change. It's still true.

Everyone since Adam and Eve has known the difference between good and evil, and everyone since Adam and Eve has chosen to do something evil.

In other words, "all have sinned and fallen short of the glory of God" (Romans 3:23).

Adam and Eve were sentenced to death for their sin, and so are we.

So is it not our fault, is it really Adam and Eve's fault that we have to die?

Yes and no. We were born with a sinful nature because all the people before us, starting with Adam and Eve, had a sinful nature. So in that sense it could be said that it was their fault.

But we have all had many choices in our life, to do good or evil, and we have ourselves chosen evil many times, and thus we have violated God's laws and disobeyed Him.

Thus we are sentenced to death...because of Adam and Eve, *and* because of us.

God could have left it at that. Live a life that is, relatively speaking, rather short, then die and be buried in the ground. Decay into dust, and that's the end of that.

There are some people who really believe that's the way it is.

But it's not, because God did not want the people He so lovingly created to have just that. He wanted to restore the relationship to the one He had originally with our ancestors, Adam and Eve.

That meant, though, that He had to make a way for us to get rid of the sin that sentenced us to death. He is perfect and holy... it was us, His created beings, that had to be cleansed of the sin that doomed us.

So He sent His Son, Jesus Christ, to take our place, to take our sentence of death, so that the death we die here is not final, but is the beginning of eternal life with Him.

But here is the part that a lot of people misunderstand: God gave us this chance, this reprieve from our death sentence, but He did not throw a figurative blanket over all of mankind and declare them free of sin.

In other words, not everyone is going to heaven when they die.

It's a free gift of an awesome loving God, but it must be acknowledged and accepted.

He gave us a choice.

And while it seems totally foolish to choose death over life, that is exactly what most people have done, are doing, and will continue to do.

It really makes you scratch your head, doesn't it?

But then, what have *you* chosen? Death or life?

The physical death we all will experience can be the last one, if we choose to accept God's gift of life, or there can be another one after that, an eternal experience of death, a separation forever from our Creator.

One thing that makes the inevitability of death a lot easier to accept is that this life we live here is not always so great. We live in a world of sin and sinners, and there are a lot of bad things going on. Life here, as much as we hang on to it, is not always that much fun, is it?

In fact, when some people die it is a relief, even to those who are close to them, because they have been going through some serious suffering.

Although you will get my dad's entire story later in this book, I have to tell you here that it was like that at the end of his life. My dad loved to talk, and he loved to eat, and at the end of his life he couldn't do either because the radiation treatments had destroyed his ability to swallow or speak.

So he was anxious for it to be over, because he wasn't enjoying his time here very much, and because he knew that where he was going after he died there would be no more pain or difficulty, only joy.

And yet, when all is said and done, we don't like to think about the inescapable fact that we, as well as every single person we know and love, are someday going to die. Though it is absolutely true, we choose to distract ourselves from contemplating what that means.

We are reminded, though, over and over again. We read an obituary in the newspaper or online, or we attend the funeral of someone we know, and while we feel and express sympathy for the family of the one who died, we also think about ourselves and our loved ones.

We are all going to die.

We can say "if something happens to me...", but the truth is, something *is* going to happen to you someday. You're going to die. You just don't know when.

When people use that phrase with me, and if I know them well enough, sometimes I'll say "what do you mean IF?". There is usually this kind of uncomfortable laugh when I ask that question.

It is important, I believe, to embrace the inevitability of death, to not just accept it but to face it.

It is important, I believe, to not just realize it will happen, but to think about what it means.

It is most important, I believe, to not just plan on it, but to plan *for* it.

The reason is because another death after that, a far worse death, is optional. If you wish you could avoid this one, knowing you can't, you will definitely want to avoid the one after that, especially knowing you can.

The end of your life here on earth, your inevitable death, though you don't know when that will be, can, and does, make sense.

# Chapter 14

# TIMEKEEPER

"Show me, O Lord, my life's end and the number of my days; let me know how fleeting is my life. You have made my days a mere handbreadth; the span of my years is as nothing before you. Each man's life is but a breath."

Psalm 39:4-5


"For you created my inmost being; you knit me together in my mother's womb. I praise you because I am fearfully and wonderfully made; your works are wonderful, I know that full well. My frame was not hidden from you when I was made in the secret place.
When I was woven together in the depths of the earth, your eyes saw my unformed body. All the days ordained for me were written in your book before one of them came to be."

Psalm 139:13-16


"Now listen, you who say, "Today or tomorrow we will go to this or that city, spend a year there, carry on business and make money.""

Why, you do not even know what will happen tomorrow. What is your life? You are a mist that appears for a little while and then vanishes."

James 4:13-14

For nearly all of my adult life the abortion issue has raged in America.

And I do believe I'm right when I use the word "raged". People who favor it will indeed rage at you if you try to have a rational discussion about it.

I know a lady like this, and on occasion the topic comes up, and her entire demeanor becomes defensive and angry. Sometimes I wonder whether this is something she experienced in her past.

Regardless, this lady, who we'll call Barb, believes abortion is justified because she believes two things. She believes that an unborn baby is not a person, not a life, and that therefore abortion is not murder. She also believes that a woman has a "right" to choose whether to have a baby or not.

Where I get myself in trouble is when I ask her for the basis of those two beliefs.

Because there is no basis. It is convenient to believe those two things if you are in favor of abortion.

Where I get myself in further trouble is when I ask her if she believes that she was created by God, because she always says she does. Then, of course, I ask her who has the authority about all matters of life and death, the Creator or the created, and now I'm really on the bad side of her because she cannot answer either way.

If she says the Creator has the authority then her position on abortion defies that authority.

If she says the created has the authority, she cannot produce any evidence that God has passed it on to His created ones.

Defying the authority of God is an impossible position to defend.

Barb is not alone. A lot of people believe that there is a God, and that He created them, and a lot of those people believe that the right to end the life of an unborn baby belongs to the woman in whose body this child resides.

I can only conclude that they don't know God for who He really is.

But now here's the interesting part. Barb's mother died, well into her 70's, and Barb mourned the loss of her mother "at such a young age".

She even asked me why I thought God would "take" her mother when she had so much life left to live.

I told her the simple truth:

God is the Timekeeper, and He knows best.

There were lots of other things I could have said, but not in the middle of her raw grief. She was wounded enough without me opening up other ones.

But her inability to understand and accept God's authority in these matters has given her the same inner conflict at her mother's death as exists when she talks about her position on abortion.

Her mother did not *choose* to die, and Barb did not choose for her mother to die, and no other human being chose to end her mother's life, yet she did die. But if Barb grants God the authority over life and death, and the time we get here on earth in this life, then she will have to change her position on abortion.

The conflict will continue until she resolves it by accepting the truth and surrendering to the authority of God.

Some people never resolve it in this life. Unfortunately they will after this life is over, when it's too late.

God is the Timekeeper of our life, and everyone's life, and quite frankly, we are not all that comfortable with it.

Why?

Mostly because we are not ready.

Why are we not ready?

I believe there are two reasons. The first is because we are uncertain about what's going to happen after we die, and the second is because we are not too comfortable with the relationship we have with the Timekeeper.

It's strange, really, why anyone would have any uncertainty about what will happen when they die, because God so clearly lays out the two possibilities: we could live eternally with Him in heaven, with no pain or sadness or anxiety, or we could be in torment, forever separated from Him, in hell.

He also makes it clear that we get to choose which we prefer, but the choice must be made now, during our life on earth.

Not only that, but He tells us that we can *know* which it will be.

If you believe that He is your Creator and Authority, and that He sent His Son, Jesus Christ, to this earth to die on the cross for the forgiveness of your sins, and if you repent of those sins and surrender your life to Him, you will spend eternity with Him.

In other words, you must accept Jesus as your Savior, and also as your *Lord*. This means your life is lived for Him, not for you.

And as I said in previous chapters, this means your life has meaning every day.

If you deny your Creator or the Son He sent to save you, you have to answer for your sins before Him at the Day of Judgment. Those sins, uncovered and unforgiven, will doom you to eternal separation from God.

Since you know which of these you are, you can and should have no uncertainty about your destination after you die.

I used to wonder why anyone would not choose to spend eternity with God, but I have since learned that not everyone would like being with Him forever. If you know God you will love God, but if you don't know Him, and don't want to know Him, you wouldn't have the desire to be with Him forever.

I really hope that's not you.

And that brings us to the second reason people are not too comfortable with God as the Timekeeper: a less than excellent relationship with Him.

Leave it to my third-grade Sunday School boys to put that into perspective.

We were reading and discussing the parable Jesus told in Luke 12:16-21. It's about a rich man who had an absolutely bumper crop, the best of all time. In fact, it was so great that he had no place to store it all. So the man decided to tear down his barns and build bigger ones to store all of his grain and all of his possessions.

But then the man made this statement: "I'll say to myself, "You have plenty of good things laid up for many years. Take life easy; eat, drink and be merry.""

But that night, right after the man made that statement, God called him a "fool", and told him that his time was up and his life was over, and all his stuff would go to someone else. All that hard work to build up all that wealth was for nothing in the end.

Now there are lots of lessons in that parable, but to me the greatest lesson is about being ready.

I asked the boys, "Was that man ready to meet God?"

"No!" they all responded.

Then one of them said, "You know, if we never know when our life will end, we need to be ready all the time."

Another then said, "You know, there are times I am doing things that I would not want to be doing when Jesus comes for me."

Still another boy picked it up from there. "I think we should make sure that we never do something we would be ashamed of if Jesus came for us, because we never know when that will be."

"Let's make a pact!" said another.

So we did. A stack of hands in the middle of the table, and together we asked God to help us live so that we would never be ashamed, no matter when He comes for us.

That is a prayer we all should pray.

If you have a poor relationship or no relationship with God, it is, and should be, of concern to you that your time may be up before you have done something about that relationship. God is a very personal God, and He has done all that He can do to have a great personal relationship with you.

The rest is up to you.

But if that relationship is not what it should be, there is no good time for your life to end.

On the other hand, if you know your destination and your relationship with God is strong, you give very little, if any, thought to when your life will end. Not only do you trust God, who knows all and decides all, but you also know you will be much better off when this life ends and you are with Him.

Perhaps there is one other source of discomfort in the truth that God is the Timekeeper.

We are not in control. God is.

Where this discomfort really manifests itself is that we spend a lot of time trying to figure out why God gives some people lots and lots of time, and others almost no time at all.

Why does God allow some people to die so young?

Actually, the answer to that question is simple.

I don't know.

Very funny, you're thinking. That's not an answer!

But it really is.

God's thinking is so far beyond ours that we could not possibly understand how He maps out the time we will each spend here. For all we know there are a million reasons why it was time for someone to die.

Oh sure, we think we can figure out some of them. The person was really sick and suffering, and God had compassion on them. Or the person was really old and had lived a "full life". Or the person had a very hard life, and God is giving them a better one. Or a person always lived in honor of God, and He was rewarding them.

While all of these reasons we can think up might be true, it's certainly true that God knows *all* the reasons, and makes the perfect decision about our time on earth long before we are ever born.

If God told us in advance how much time we had, if He revealed to us the exact moment when our life would end, our lives might be quite different, wouldn't they?

Something to think about....

No, actually, the "not knowing" part is really the good part. God, who created us and knows us intimately, and who has all knowledge and all power and who is ever present, made the perfect decision a long time ago, and He doesn't tell us because He wants us to trust Him with this.

Because we can, you know.

And while there are some people, many people really, who are uncomfortable with God as the Timekeeper, there are some who are very happy that He is.

These are people who, if a car ran a red light and smashed into them, or if someone walked up to them with a gun and shot them, or if they were diagnosed with a terminal illness, would be fine with that, because they would *know* that the God they know so well, and trust so much, and love so dearly, was allowing it.

Whether you choose to believe it or not, God is the Timekeeper. The longer you live in denial of that absolute truth, the more frightened and anxious you will become, and the harder it will be to face the end of your life, or that of your loved ones.

It will also be hard to justify some of the things you have done, or that you claim to believe.

That's where Jesus comes in with forgiveness and grace.

When you accept and embrace God as the One who decides when your life will be over, you will have nothing to fear, and much to do while you are still here.

And maybe, just maybe, God will, when you are eternally with Him, explain to you why the timing of your death was so perfect.

Because it will be, you know...He will see to it.

Make sure you are ready.

# Chapter 15

# AVERSION

"Remember how fleeting is my life. For what futility you have created all men!
What man can live and not see death, or save himself from the power of the grave?"

Psalm 89:47-48

As a father has compassion on his children, so the Lord has compassion on those who fear him; for he knows how we are formed, he remembers that we are dust. As for man, his days are like grass, he flourishes like a flower of the field; the wind blows over it and it is gone, and its place remembers it no more."

Psalm 103:13-16

"All go to the same place; all come from dust, and to dust all return."

Ecclesiastes 3:20

Although it was some 15 years ago, I remember it well.
Flying home from Hawaii, our plane was about an hour out of Honolulu, over the Pacific Ocean. The pilot came on the intercom and announced in a very calm voice that one of the engines was burning through a "great deal" of fuel, and that he had to shut it down.

Although, he said, we did in fact have enough fuel to make it safely to the West Coast and that the aircraft could fly without that engine, he felt it would be wiser to turn back and return to Honolulu.

Interestingly, everyone in the plane knew that this was a very experienced pilot. They had announced before we left that this was his last flight before retirement. I could tell, too, that he chose his words very carefully and spoke very confidently. The last thing he needed was a panic among the passengers.

And indeed, there was no panic, but I got the sense that there were a lot of rather nervous people on that plane. You could almost see the passengers wheels turning in their minds, thinking about things undone and words unsaid. A lot of people looked at their watches every few minutes. It was a long hour.

It was an especially long hour for me. Not so much because I was envisioning crashing into the Pacific Ocean, although I will admit I breathed a quiet prayer to God.

I didn't like the idea of never seeing my son again.

At the same time I was at peace with whatever happened, and after putting it in God's hands I relaxed.

But not for long.

No, the reason it was a long hour for me was the elderly lady sitting next to me. I first recognized her panic and fear when she dug her fingernails into my arm on the armrest between us. After unpeeling her fingers I held her hand and looked at her, and the look in her eyes told me all I needed to know.

She was deathly afraid...or should I say she was afraid of death.

"Are we going to die?" she asked me.

"Someday, yes," I answered, "but I don't think it will be today."

She relaxed somewhat and then asked, "How do you know that?"

"I don't, only God does," I said, "but I really don't think this is all that serious a problem for Him to handle."

She relaxed a little more, but kept her hand on my arm. It seemed to help, and I didn't mind as long as she kept her fingernails out of my skin.

She did very well until we began to approach the runway at Honolulu, and we could all see the lineup of emergency vehicles with lights flashing on either side of the runway. I think we all had the same two thoughts at the same time: (1)is this more serious than we thought? and (2)is there going to be a problem landing this plane?

The nervousness returned...so did the fingernails.

We landed without a problem, and a few hours later boarded a different plane. I was actually somewhat surprised to see that the elderly lady boarded as well.

I have thought about that lady a lot over the years. She was well along in years, and had to know that sooner rather than later she would die, and yet she had a powerful aversion to dying. She knew she could not avoid death, but that is exactly what she wished to do.

Illogical, isn't it?

And very, very common.

We don't want to think about it and we don't want to be reminded of it. It's as if not thinking about it means it won't happen to us or to anyone we love.

But it's like an elephant in the room, and we're talking about the lovely painting on the wall.

We know that death, ours and everyone else's, is inevitable. We know that we have a limited amount of time on this earth, and that God is the Timekeeper.

And still we have this aversion to it.

Some people will tell you that they are not uncomfortable with the idea of their death, and that their aversion is not to death, but to the *dying* part. To a certain degree, and in the case of a few people, I guess I can buy that, but I believe most people who say this are in serious denial.

Others will tell you that they are not uncomfortable with the idea of their death, but just not *now*. Again, there are probably a few with whom this is actually true, but again, I think most are denying reality.

I've never taken a poll on this, not even one of my completely unscientific, ask-whoever-I-see-for-the-next-two-weeks kind of polls, but I have to believe that a very great majority of people have an aversion to death.

There are a number of reasons for this aversion.

The first is that it is something we do not control. We like to be in control, at least of everything in our own lives. We have convinced ourselves that this is when we are happy, when we are in control.

Some people like to be in control of not only their own life, but others as well, so the idea of even someone they know dying is out of the question. This upsets their view of the world as it revolves around them.

Sound like someone you know? Hopefully it's not you.

Even people who understand and accept that God controls this are sometimes frustrated at His timing (which, by the way, is perfect).

Another reason for aversion to death is that to many people it is an unknown. They don't know what is going to happen when they die, so they automatically fear it and do everything in their power to postpone it as long as possible.

And despite the fact that loved ones have died, and they don't know what happened to those loved ones after they died, they have never done any research into what *does* happen when someone dies.

Because they might not like what they found...for their loved ones *or* for themselves.

A third reason people have an aversion to death is that they *do* know what happens when someone dies, and they know they are not ready.

They know that the time for them to choose to surrender their life to their Creator will have run out. They know that they will have to stand before Him and be judged by Him solely on the merits of their life.

A life devoted to them and their happiness, not a life devoted to God.

No wonder they have an aversion to death.

But if God gets to choose the time of your death, and you know this, why would you continue to postpone giving your life to Him?

There are also a number of ways you can see this aversion to death in people, and maybe even in yourself.

One is the person who grieves forever.

We all know people like this, people who continue to grieve for years and years after a loved one has died, revisiting it and wallowing in it to the point where they become a difficult person to be around.

They think about the injustice of it, even in cases when the person was very old or very sick. They dwell on the effect this has had on them, their loneliness and emptiness without this person they loved.

They wonder where God was when this happened, as if He was distracted and failed to notice. Or they question His wisdom at choosing this time, leaving them with a ruined life and nonstop grief.

They have chosen a life that seems focused on death, when in fact they have chosen a life that denies the reality and practicality of a death timed perfectly by God.

Then there is the person who avoids death every way they can.

I saw this recently in someone I know pretty well. A man she had known for many years, but who had moved away and who she had not seen recently, died very unexpectedly and at a relatively young age.

When I asked her if she was going to the visitation or the funeral, she answered quickly, perhaps too quickly.

"No, I really didn't know him that well and haven't seen him for a long time."

This got me to thinking. In all the years I've known this woman I could only think of two funerals she went to, and both were ones in which her absence would have been very noticeable and very difficult, if not impossible, to explain.

Knowing her as I do, it makes me wonder if her aversion to death has to do with her discomfort with her life and her relationship with the Timekeeper.

I don't know, and probably it's not important if I do, but I know God knows.

A third type of person in whom you can see aversion to death is the one who will not talk about it.

This person will usually do one of two things. They will either change the subject immediately, or they will make a joke about it. The joke will then lead to changing the subject.

Oddly enough, I believe this is a person who in their private moments thinks about death a lot. Their life leads them to wonder what God will do with them when that life is over. God, I believe, challenges people like this to examine where they are in their relationship with Him even when they don't want to.

Here's the really odd thing, the *real* elephant in the room: the same people who will tell you that they believe that a loving God will not send people to hell for eternity have this death aversion.

"Wait a minute," you're saying. "If they don't believe that God will send them to hell, then they must believe that God will bring them into heaven with Him. Wouldn't that make death a good thing?"

You would certainly think so. But most, if not all, of the people who say they believe this know in their heart it's not true. God makes them aware of the fact that their choice to love Him and live in obedience to Him or live in opposition to Him will ultimately decide their destination after they die.

There are even churches who will teach this, and people flock to these churches to hear this lie, because they so desperately want it to be true.

And yet God reminds them it is not true, and their aversion to death will not go away.

There are people who do not have an aversion to death.

While they may not be crazy about the dying part, especially if it involves pain or loss of dignity, they trust the One who is in control of all of these things.

They have put their faith and trust in Jesus Christ as their Lord and Savior.

They know that when they die they will go to be with Him forever, just as He promised, and they are very excited about that kind of future. To leave this life is to go to be with the Lord to whom they have given their life.

It wasn't always like that with them. They knew at one point in their life that they were destined to die and be doomed to answer for their sin in this life before a perfect and holy God at the Judgment.

But they learned that God had made a way for them, through the sacrifice of His own Son, Jesus Christ, on a cross, to wash away their sins so that He would not hold those sins against them.

They learned that the way to access this forgiveness was to bow before this Jesus, to acknowledge Him as the Son of God, to ask for forgiveness for their sins, and to surrender their life in this world to Him that they might have eternal life with Him when this brief life is over.

Now they have no doubt, and they have no aversion to death. It is the doorway to life.

It's an awesome plan, isn't it? Of all the things God controls and we don't, He gives us the control over this one.

The really big one.

I call that grace.

Want to unload that concern you have, that aversion to death?

God has made a way.

# Chapter 16

# POSTPONEMENT

"Rend your heart and not your garments. Return to the Lord your God, for he is gracious and compassionate, slow to anger and abounding in love, and he relents from sending calamity."

Joel 2:13

"Who is a God like you, who pardons sin and forgives the transgression of the remnants of his inheritance? You do not stay angry forever but delight to show mercy."

Micah 7:18

"But do not forget this one thing, dear friends: With the Lord a day is like a thousand years, and a thousand years are like a day. The Lord is not slow in keeping his promise, as some understand slowness. He is patient with you, not wanting anyone to perish, but everyone to come to repentance."

II Peter 3:8-9

There is a document you should have in place, and if you don't I would recommend you get one.

It's called a Health Care Power-of-Attorney, and I recommend that each of my clients prepare one. It's a legal form so it is best to have it done by an attorney, but it is not absolutely necessary. You can obtain the form, and have it properly witnessed and notarized to make it legal.

The document includes some questions about your health care preferences in certain specific circumstances, but more importantly, it designates a person who you have chosen to make your health care decisions for you in the event that you cannot. It even asks you to choose an alternate person in the event your first choice cannot, for a variety of reasons, do so.

It is not only an important document, but an interesting exercise to complete. It not only requires you to decide who you trust enough to literally put your life in their hands, but also to decide to what degree you want to try to postpone your death.

Choosing the person can be challenging. For most married people, their spouse is the obvious first choice as their primary agent, but I have seen cases where spouses don't trust each other enough to grant them this power. I could tell you some really interesting stories about some of the discussions *that* sparks, but that would divert us from the main point here.

For nearly everyone, choosing the alternate person is more difficult. I must admit it took me a while, but I finally chose my sister, who thinks a lot like I do. I told her not to rush me out of this world, but not to delay my trip to heaven, either. She understood perfectly.

It is very interesting and even eye-opening to discuss this with people. Some firmly desire to have nothing done to prolong their life if it is, and will continue to be, devoid of quality. Others want everything under the sun and known to man done to prolong their life and postpone their death.

And although I think I know the answer in either case, I still love to ask them *why* that is their wish.

They will tell me all kinds of things. Those that want to postpone as long as possible talk about everything from a miraculous and unexplained recovery to a sudden medical breakthrough in research. Those that want little or nothing done to prolong their life will usually mention the burden of time and money placed on their loved ones.

Yet it is what they *don't* tell me that is really driving their decision.

It is their relationship with God.

It is the knowledge, regardless of what they may tell you, that they will no longer be in control of anything once they leave this life, and that they will be meeting God face to face. Their future, their eternity, will be in His hands.

I know what you're saying right now. You're saying that some people don't believe there is a God, that when they die that is it, it's all over.

But I'm here to tell you I don't believe them.

As people get older, and therefore closer to death, the awareness of God's existence, which He, their Creator, puts in them, is heightened.

They know...He makes sure of that.

And that is why they want to postpone death as long as possible. They are going to meet the One who created all the incredible things they see around them, on the earth and in the sky and beyond, and who also purposely created them down to the last detail.

That is a God with a *lot* of power, and they have denied His very existence during their time on earth. Meeting Him is something they would really like to put off as long as possible. To say it makes them uncomfortable is an understatement.

On the other hand, the people who don't want to prolong their life on this earth have a different perspective.

Admittedly some of them simply don't want to suffer any pain, or don't want to lose their dignity. They don't like the thought of people, especially those close to them, seeing them in those circumstances.

But most of this group wants to begin their *real* life, their eternal life, and they know that once this life is over, then they get to meet their Creator, and their Savior, Jesus Christ, who they love.

And while they're not in a hurry to leave, they do look forward to the next life, because they know what it will be like.

They know the place where they're going after they die, and it is driving the way they are living every day in this life.

The bottom line is, if you have a close relationship with God, you are not concerned with death, and may even consider it with joyful anticipation. If you do not have a close relationship with God, death is something you would like to postpone as long as you possibly can.

But while some people want to postpone their death as long as possible, and others don't, pretty much everyone wants to postpone the death of those they love.

Whether it's spouses, children, parents, grandparents, close friends, or relatives of close friends, we wish for them to live and live and live...and not die.

We take extraordinary action to prolong their lives, every-thing in our power, in fact, dreading the idea of life without them.

Some of these actions are simple.

We buckle our children into car seats and seat belts to protect them in the car.

We take children or parents or grandparents to the doctor when they are ill, wanting to cure whatever ails them as quickly as possible.

We put locks on our doors to protect our family.

We feed our children healthy food, not just for health now, but to establish a pattern for them for the future. We warn them about things that are bad for them.

We put elderly people in the best environment we can find to prolong their life, where there is 24-hour expert care.

We pray for them to have a long life.

Postponement of the death of a loved one seems like such a good idea, doesn't it?

But when it comes right down to it, that wish, that prayer, that no one we are close to will die, is a selfish one. It is because our sorrow would be great, our grief would be unbearable, and our life would be empty.

I know of people, and I'm sure you do, too, who have fervently prayed that their elderly loved one would live on, despite the pain and suffering and indignity this person was enduring.

What is really interesting is that all of this talk about postponement implies that we actually have the power to postpone death, ours or someone else's.

We don't.

Oh, I know we think we do, and we believe that actions we are taking or decisions we are making is doing that, but it just isn't so.

God makes those decisions. He decides, according to Psalm 139, the number of our days before we are ever born.

God chooses the day we begin this life, and He chooses the day we will end this life. Nothing we do to try to change the day of our death will affect His decision. His wisdom is perfect, and therefore His timing is perfect.

There are times, aren't there, when we really wonder about that. People we love die young, and we are looking for an explanation. We are wondering about the wisdom of a death of one so young.

There usually is no explanation, primarily because we are incapable of understanding it if He gave it to us. Sometimes He gives us little parts of it later, when we are ready and capable of understanding.

The Giver of Life, our Creator, is the one best equipped to choose when it will end.

And while I don't know, and am incapable of understanding, how He makes that decision for each one of us, I do know this: He often postpones the day of our death in the hope that we will repent of our sins and accept His free gift of salvation.

It's called mercy.

Our God, our Creator, loves each one of us so much that He wishes to spend eternity with us, and He waits and waits and waits for us to turn to Him with the same kind of love.

And He knows us so well that He knows exactly when we have made our final decision.

He knows what is in our hearts.

He knows what is in the very depths of our soul.

He knows when a person has decided to accept Him by their decision to acknowledge His Son as their Lord and Savior, to repent of their sins against Him, and to surrender their will in this life to His.

This person does not need their death to be postponed. Their gift of eternal life is assured. Their place in heaven is reserved.

He can choose the date of their departure from this life for His glory...and they will be fine with that.

Have you ever known anyone like that? I have.

God also knows when a person has decided to reject Him with no possibility of that ever changing.

There is no reason to postpone that person's death, either. They have made their choice to be separated from Him forever.

But God also knows when a person who is resisting Him has not made that their final decision.

And for that person, He is willing and able and likely to postpone their death to give them a chance to turn to Him. Not only will He wait for them, but He will put people in their life to make His love for them known to them. He will even sometimes do miraculous things in their lives to draw them to Him. At times He will even put trials in their life so that they will turn to Him.

God will definitely do whatever He can to give each of the precious ones He created and loves the opportunity to accept His incredible grace.

Mercy...from a God who has the power by His words alone to create all we can see, and a great deal that we can't.

How can you not love a God with that kind of love and compassion?

When I think about this, I always end up thinking about Jesus' parable about the fig tree in Luke 13. In the parable, there is a man with a fig tree which had not produced any fruit for three years, and he ordered it cut down. But the man who cared for his trees asked him to give it one more year, saying that he would give it special attention in that year, that he would water and fertilize it. If after that year of special attention it still did not bear fruit, then he would agree to cut it down.

That, my friends, is our merciful God. He'll give us one more year, with special attention, so that we will not be cut down.

Postponement...by grace.

He will give us every chance, but He will not make the decision for us.

And our days are numbered.

# Chapter 17

# HOPE

"Therefore we are always confident and know that as long as we are at home in the body we are away from the Lord. We live by faith, not by sight. We are confident, I say, and would prefer to be away from the body and at home with the Lord."

II Corinthians 5:6-8

"Because God wanted to make the unchanging nature of his purpose very clear to the heirs of what was promised, he confirmed it with an oath. God did this so that, by two unchangeable things in which it is impossible for God to lie, we who have fled to take hold of the hope offered to us may be greatly encouraged. We have this hope as an anchor for the soul, firm and secure."

Hebrews 6:17-19a

"We know that the whole creation has been groaning as in the pains of childbirth right up to the present time. Not only so, but we ourselves, who have the firstfruits of the Spirit, groan inwardly as we wait eagerly for our adoption as sons, the redemption of our bodies. For in this hope we were saved. But hope that is seen is no hope at all. Who hopes for what he already has? But if we hope for what we do not yet have, we wait for it patiently."

Romans 8:22-25

Talk about your good news, bad news situations…this was a doozy.

You see, we have this neighbor, an older lady, who, like us, has a very big yard. For the first few years after we moved into our house she had a lawn service that came on a regular basis to cut the grass, trim trees and bushes, remove fallen branches and whatever else needed to be done.

One day I noticed a small lawn tractor sitting outside by her garage door, so I went over and asked her if it was hers and why it was out there. I thought she might be selling it since she never used it, and mine was getting pretty old.

She told me it was hers, but that she got it out to get it serviced, because she was going to cut her own grass from now on. She had decided the lawn service was too expensive.

I must admit I was pretty startled to hear this, considering her age and the size of her yard. However, the first thing I thought of when she told me this was the hill in her back yard. It is very, very steep, and no doubt a very tricky part to mow.

So I asked her, "How are you going to cut the grass on the hill in back?"

Her reply was a classic: "I'll just close my eyes and hold on tight."

"No," I replied emphatically. "I'll cut your grass for you."

And so, for quite a few years now, I have cut her grass and done the necessary trimming work in her yard. She insisted that I use her lawn tractor on her yard, which seemed only fair to me, as well.

But there was one problem: that hill. The problem was that her small lawn tractor didn't have the power to cut the grass going *up* the hill. I would get halfway up and then have to back down again. Cutting it going *down* the hill was also a problem, because the hill was so steep that the brakes couldn't hold the tractor, and eventually the tractor went flying down the hill with me on it. I can tell you that was scary every time.

My solution? Cut the grass by backing down the hill. The tractor went very slowly in reverse, and never picked up speed.

It was a great plan, and was working well...until that one day a few years ago.

The good news: I was almost done. I just had to make one more pass down the hill.

The bad news: As I was backing down the hill, the chute tangled itself into a thick patch of weeds. Instead of tearing right through those weeds it caught, and the mower kept going while the chute did not. Unfortunately the mower started to go sideways, and I knew if it went completely sideways on a hill that steep the mower would tip over.

The good news: I could see what was happening so I let off the gas and turned off the mower blades.

The bad news: That was all I had time to do. It went sideways and tipped over downhill. Despite my best effort to get off and free of the tractor it landed on my left leg.

The good news: It was still a small lawn tractor, and not as heavy as some, and I was able to get my leg out from under it.

The bad news: It hurt...a lot.

The good news: I could walk on it, and I was able to make it to the top of the hill, where I promptly sat down.

The bad news: Now it really hurt.

The good news: My neighbor came running out right away, and she is a retired nurse.

The bad news: She slammed a hard ice pack on my painfully bruised shin bone.

I could go on, as you can about imagine, but I think you get my point. As bad and as frightening as that experience was, there was good news. My leg was not broken, I was not trapped under the mower for hours, and I did not lose any body parts to a still spinning mower blade.

Not to mention the lesson I learned....

I have since bought myself a new lawn tractor, a very powerful one at that, and I drive a nice sloping path down to the lower part of her yard, and cut the grass on that hill driving up the hill.

In almost every situation in life, there is good news and there is bad news.

You can choose to focus on either one. We all know people who are generally optimistic, and we know people who are pessimistic. We know people who will look for the silver lining around every cloud, and people who can find a dark cloud inside every silver lining.

But when it comes to death, most people can't see any good news. They don't see a silver lining.

I'm here to tell you there is good news...very good news.

It's called hope.

The dictionary defines hope as "a desire accompanied by expectation of or belief in fulfillment."

As is true with all desires, it is one we can choose or reject.

As is true with all expectation or belief, we can choose to believe or not to believe.

The problem with hope is that it is usually something we desire that is outside our control. We may hope for a promotion at work, but it is not our decision. We may hope to win a competition that has judges, but it is not our decision.

If we knew, however, that the outcome would be in our favor, we would certainly view it with far greater hope.

And that is actually how it is with death. Even as most people see no hope in death, there is actually greater certainty of hope in death than in anything we will ever experience in life.

The hope in death is rooted in the promises of God. God has told us the whole plan. He has laid out and explained for us what will happen when we die, and has told us that we can choose eternal life, and that once we make that choice we have a hope that no one can ever take away.

If you read every Bible verse that contains the word hope, you will certainly understand that, though you will find yourself trusting in a future you cannot see nor totally comprehend, that future has the personal guarantee of the God that created you and everything you see around you.

You know, the God who keeps every promise.

The God who has *all* power and *all* knowledge.

The God who is everywhere all the time.

The God who has authority over everything in heaven and earth.

The God who is holy and perfect and just.

What He has promised is that death is the doorway to a life so much better than the one we work so hard to hang on to here that we do not have an imagination big enough to begin to picture it.

That's a pretty good foundation for hope, wouldn't you say?

You may have a good life, generally speaking, and be pretty content right now, but the one thing we all know is that it won't last. At some point in this life, and in this sinful world, there will be bad news to go with the good news.

We also know that this life itself won't last. At some point we are all going to die.

If Jesus Christ is your personal Lord and Savior, if you have chosen to accept God's free gift of grace and salvation, you will be able to hold on to the hope that no matter what comes your way in this life, death will take you to the next one, one with no bad news of any kind.

And oh yes, it will, by the way, last forever.

God has guaranteed that we can have this desire accompanied by an expectation of fulfillment...this hope.

There are, of course, people with no hope. They believe that there is no God, and have lived their life accordingly. They live their life moment by moment, believing that they better get all they can out of this life because when they die, that is it. It's all over.

There is only fleeting hope in life for these people, and no hope at all in death.

These are miserable people.

You know some of them don't you? So do I.

I pray you aren't one of them.

There are also people with false hope. They believe that God will take them to heaven when they die because they were a "good person", or because they tried to live a good life and be nice and helpful to everyone, or because they think God would not condemn them to hell because He is a loving God.

They believe this, and live with this false hope, because they found someone who they believe to be intelligent to tell them this, and they want to believe it. They do not know, and perhaps don't want to know, what God Himself has said.

These are not the happiest people, either. Their foundational beliefs are quicksand, based on words spoken by men and women who will eventually let them down. Their hope is a delusion, and God will not let them get comfortable with it. He wants them to know the truth, and to respond to it.

I believe that a lot of the people who live with this false hope do so because they have seen loved ones die and there have been questions in their mind about the eternal destiny of this loved one. They know that if what they have chosen to believe is not true, then their loved one is in hell.

So they seek out a church that will tell them that this loved one is in heaven. They do not wish to address the reality of a God who is perfect in love and in justice. They want to be made to feel better about the passing of this loved one.

It is a dangerous risk they are taking...eternally dangerous.

Do you know anyone like this? I'm sure you do. I know lots of them.

I pray that you are not one of them, either.

Then there are the people who not only have hope, but they have good reason for it. They have given this life over to God, through His Son, Jesus Christ, because they know God's plan for eternity. They know that this life has its brief time, and that when God decides that their life now is over, they will walk through the doorway that death provides into an indescribably beautiful eternal life with Him.

It is admittedly difficult for people who live with no hope or with false hope to understand these people who find hope in death. They are content with whatever situation they are in, and more than willing to allow God to dictate not only their life here, but their life hereafter, including when it should begin.

It really comes down to knowing God personally. If you know Him, you will trust Him.

In everything...even death.

Perhaps there is a lot of good news in your life right now. Though I'm glad for you, I pray that you will not find hope in that. It is fleeting. I think you know that.

Consider all the good news in your life as a blessing from God, a reminder that He is there and is involved, and is able to do this and much more for you.

He wants you to find your hope in Him.

Perhaps there is a lot of bad news in your life right now. I don't wish it on you, but pray that you will not lose hope because of it.

Consider all the bad news that God has allowed in your life as nothing compared to the life He has promised after this one is over. Think about whether it might be possible that He is reminding you that He still wants you as His child, and wants you to trust Him to save you.

He wants you to have hope.

He has personally guaranteed it.

Even in death.

Now that's good news.

# Chapter 18

# JERRY'S STORY

"For none of us lives to himself alone and none of us dies to himself alone.
If we live, we live to the Lord; and if we die, we die to the Lord. So, whether we live or die, we belong to the Lord. For this very reason, Christ died and returned to life so that he might be the Lord of both the dead and the living."

Romans 14:7-9

"For I know that through your prayers and the help given by the Spirit of Jesus Christ, what has happened to me will turn out for my deliverance. I eagerly expect and hope that I will in no way be ashamed, but will have sufficient courage so that now as always Christ will be exalted in my body, whether by life or by death. For to me, to live is Christ and to die is gain."

Philippians 1:19-21

"Even though I walk through the valley of the shadow of death I will fear no evil, for you are with me."

Psalm 23:4

No one will ever write a book about my father, Jerry Walston. He was not famous, or rich, or powerful. He lived a life that was largely unnoticed and, by the standards of the world we live in, unimportant.

But as it turned out, by God's grace and guidance, his life had quite an impact on many people.

And his death had an even greater impact.

Jerry grew up in the small (and I do mean small!) farming communities of southwest Iowa. Probably the greatest influence on him as a young boy at home was his mother, who loved the Lord with all her beautiful heart.

After high school and a stint in the military, he went to school and then landed a job in a small southern Minnesota city as the engineer of a radio station, a job he held for some 30 years. It was during this period of his life that his love for his Savior, Jesus Christ, took root and grew, and his service for his Lord took shape.

He was a deeply spiritual man, and spent a lot of time in his Bible, but it didn't end there. He shared the good news of the gospel with nearly everyone he came to know, and a fair number of people he barely knew. He was instrumental in starting a church in this city, and did a great deal of the preaching until the church grew large enough to be able to afford a minister.

Jerry loved to preach, and every sermon, written out in long-hand, was from the Bible. God's Word was the basis of each sermon, and he was excellent at applying what the Bible said to the lives of those listening.

A side note: he saved every one of those sermons, and now each of his five children have some of them...quite the legacy.

Like all earthly fathers, he was imperfect. As a close observer of this, I noted the ways he fathered me and my siblings, and determined that in some ways I wanted to be a father like him, and in certain other ways I vowed to be different.

My father was an authoritative man, and liked it that way. He liked to be in charge, and he could be quite intimidating. Interestingly, God changed that trait in him as he grew older... more on that later.

He unexpectedly lost his job at the radio station in his 50's, and tried his hand at buying and operating two radio stations in Iowa, the second of which left him completely broke when he had to shut it down. It turns out he was a much better engineer than he was a businessman.

He then served for several years as the minister of a small church in a small town in Iowa.

And then, quite suddenly, he decided to stop living for the Lord and to start living for Jerry.

I will not give you the details of this, but I will tell you that his actions shocked and alienated nearly everyone who knew him, most notably his children. His decision to do what he wanted, no matter how it affected everyone else, changed our family dynamics permanently.

This was when God taught me what it meant to honor your father. Somehow, I still had to do that despite the fact that I was angry at him for his behavior. In the 11 hours it took me to drive to go talk to him, I figured it out with God's help. I was blunt in my words of truth that what he was doing was wrong, but not cruel. I reminded him that I loved him, and so did God. I asked him to reconsider the decision he had made to forsake what he knew was right.

Although he refused to reconsider his decision, that conversation kept us connected, and God in His wisdom had made it possible for me to continue to communicate with my father. I could continue to speak truth to him, and urge him to repent of his sin, receive God's forgiveness, and return to the close relationship with God he had enjoyed for all of his life.

For a number of years, this bore no fruit. He would talk to me often on the phone, but it was always about golf, or fishing, or my work. When I tried to talk to him about spiritual things, he would change the subject. He was trying very hard to avoid God.

Then one day when we were talking he asked me about a verse in the Bible, and what I thought that verse meant. The more we talked the more convinced I became that something had changed, so I asked him what had happened.

He told me that he had finally broken down and admitted to himself, and to God, that what he had done was wrong, and he was sorry for what he had done. He had asked for God's forgiveness, and, as God has promised, forgiveness was granted.

Our relationship took on a whole new direction as his heart returned to the Lord. All of our conversations were spiritual, and I marveled as I observed the growth of my dad's relationship with God, and his understanding of God's Word and God's will.

He learned a lot more and grew a lot more as a man humbled by his own foolishness than he ever did as a righteous, but proud, man.

Through this time, a number of years determined perfect by God, I gained an understanding of the spiritual perspective of my father, and grew in my own as well. I was going to find out that this understanding would be needed.

Jerry was diagnosed with cancer shortly after his 80th birthday. He had surgery to remove lumps from his neck, but only so much could be removed, and he had to have extensive radiation. Although the radiation was effective, other areas of cancer were cropping up in his body, and worse yet, the radiation made it hard (and eventually impossible) for him to swallow or talk.

During one of his times in the hospital he called me, and in his now raspy voice he said something I will never forget.

"This cancer is great," he said.

I thought I had misunderstood what he had said, so I asked him to repeat it.

He laughed. "I said this cancer is great," he repeated. "I have been telling people about Jesus all my life, and they wouldn't listen. *Now* they'll listen! They feel sorry for me because I'm sick, and when they look at me they know I'm going to die soon. Then they start thinking about what's going to happen when *they* die."

Because he was losing his voice, he asked me to send him a box of my books that he could start giving out to people as a ministry. He was very proud of the books I had written, and he wanted to use them to help people get connected with Jesus. I sent him the books, and found out that he was actually *selling* the books to them. He believed that people would more likely read a book that cost them some money. I received checks and notes from all around Iowa, and later, at his funeral, I talked to an astonishing number of people who had read my books.

The next phone call I remember well was right after the test that revealed more cancer in his body. They told him they could try to treat these areas with radiation and chemotherapy, as well, but he sensed that this was not God's will, and that his time on this earth was coming to an end.

"If it's all right with you, I think I'm just going to go home and ride it out," were his exact words.

Knowing he was very tuned in to the will of his Creator, and that he was starting to really look forward to seeing Jesus face to face, I gave him my blessing.

At home under hospice care, I knew his time was short, so I went to see him and spend a day with him. This was somewhat challenging, as he could no longer speak at all, and yet that day we had as great a communication as we had ever enjoyed.

He wrote down this question: "Do you know what you're going to say at my funeral?"

I knew he would ask this, and I had been given a lot of time to think about it, so I told him what I was going to say. He grinned from ear to ear and gave me a double thumbs-up. I can still see that grin.

We actually spent quite a bit of that day planning his funeral. That might seem weird to most people, but it wasn't to us. We both wanted his death to have impact in others' lives for the glory of God.

And we knew he was going home to be with Jesus forever. We knew it.

I read to him a bit that day. I knew just what to read that he would like. I read several of his favorite Bible passages. I read some devotions that I knew he would enjoy. I read him his favorite chapter from my first book. The story about us in that chapter made him laugh as he recalled it.

When I left I knew it would be the last time I would see him on this earth. I hugged him and kissed him, and then I looked right in his eyes and smiled as I said, "I'll see you over there."

The huge smile on his face when I said that is forever imprinted on my mind.

That was a Friday. On Saturday night he died. On Sunday I got the call. On Monday we were headed back there for his funeral.

I am going to finish this chapter with exactly the words I said at his funeral. They are my words, and they are his words, but above all, my dad and I both knew they were the words God had chosen for this moment, and for these people:

"Do not let your hearts be troubled. Trust in God; trust also in me. In my Father's house are many rooms; if it were not so, I would have told you. I am going there to prepare a place for you. And if I go and prepare a place for you, I will come back and take you to be with me that you also may be where I am. You know the way to the place where I am going. Thomas said to him, "Lord, we don't know where you are going, so how can we know the way?" Jesus answered, "I am the way and the truth and the life. No one comes to the Father except through me. If you really knew me, you would know my Father as well. From now on, you do know him and have seen him." John 14:1-7

I first agreed to do this - "preach the sermon at my funeral", as Dad so characteristically put it - about five years ago. Of course I first wanted to know if he was trying to tell me something, but discovered that God was already speaking to him about this day, about this one last opportunity for him to address, even as he sat joyfully in heaven, his family and friends about what meant the most to him: his relationship with God, and with His Son, Jesus Christ.

I must admit that a week or so after agreeing to do this, I called him back and said that I was not so sure that I could do it, but he talked me back into it. He told me that I would know best exactly what he would want said. He never changed his opinion on that. I talked to him last Friday about what I would say, and received his wholehearted approval.

So I consider it quite an honor to represent him, and more importantly the God he so loved and served, at this event that is one of both sorrow and celebration.

Sorrow at the empty spot in all of our hearts, missing him already and knowing none of our lives on this earth will be quite the same without him. Celebration that we know with the greatest of certainty that Dad is in Glory with the Savior he adores.

I want to talk about my father's legacy.

It was not one of wealth, or power, or influence, or fame...oh no, it was much more special, much deeper, than that.

My father was not perfect. When I was young, I thought he was, but I learned that he was just like me...and just like you... a sinner in need of a Savior. He was born with a sinful nature, exactly the way of all men and women since Adam and Eve. But I also learned that he had found a Savior in Jesus Christ. He was, as I'm sure you all know, quick to point this out.

On Sunday night as I grabbed my Bible for words of comfort, I opened to this passage and thought immediately of Dad.

"For in Christ all the fullness of the Deity lives in bodily form, and you have been given fullness in Christ, who is the head over every power and authority. In him you were also circumcised, in the putting off of the sinful nature, not with a circumcision done by the hands of men but with the circumcision done by Christ, having been buried with him in baptism and raised with him through your faith in the power of God, who raised him from the dead. When you were dead in your sins and in the uncircumcision of your sinful nature, God made you alive with Christ. He forgave us all our sins, having cancelled the written code, with its regulations, that was against us and that stood opposed to us; he took it away, nailing it to the cross. And having disarmed the powers and authorities, he made a public spectacle of them, triumphing over them by the cross." Colossians 2:9-15

You see, as a young man my father discovered that Jesus Christ conquered death and sin when he died on the cross and was resurrected the third day. And he realized that Jesus didn't just die for all men and women everywhere and for all time, past and present. He died for him personally. He died for Jerry Walston.

And oh, by the way, he died for me...and he died for you...personally.

This changed my dad, and through him a great many other people were changed, as well.

My father recognized his status as a hopelessly lost sinner, repented of that sin, confessed it all to God, and accepted Jesus Christ as his personal Lord and Savior.

Then, for him, the fun really began, as this changed man began to experience all the ways that God would use him. It's one thing to have God to desire to use you...it's quite another to embrace it in the way my father did.

My father really cared about people...all people of all types. Wherever he was, he ran into people he cared about.

He cared about their needs, whatever they were, but he cared most about the condition of their soul.

Sort of like Jesus, huh?

I could tell you stories of the questionable characters that he cared about...people who looked scary, talked nasty, and smelled worse.

But to him they were all souls in need of a Savior.

It was a long time before I figured out that God was working through him, and it was God who made all those outer things unimportant to my father.

His testimony was always on the front burner, no matter who you were. He was never shy about speaking of his faith, never hesitant to point people to Jesus Christ.

"I am the Way, the Truth, and the Life."

My father liked to help people, and he would help with anything, anytime.

Even people he didn't really know.

Even doing things he didn't really know how to do. He would try to figure it out. And usually he did...not always, but usually.

He didn't do it for any other reason than that he liked to help people. Granted it opened a lot of doors for his testimony, but he was just wired that way by God. He had no ulterior motive...it was just part of the new nature God gave him...a spiritual gift, if you will.

He especially liked helping his children, even when they wanted to be independent and didn't want any help. Even then, we couldn't help but love that way he had about him.

My father was a man of joy. Not always happy, but always joyful.

And it was a developing joy. I discovered it in the past 7 or 8 years, because he had developed such a strong faith in God, and he was never anxious about what God's will for him might be...he was joyful just to be a part of the plan.

We didn't really talk about joy. We talked almost exclusively about spiritual things, like what we were studying, who we were trying to help with spiritual matters, what God was doing in our lives. We did talk a lot about my books, which seemed to give him special joy.

But I noticed that with his growing closeness to God, with his ever-stronger relationship with Jesus Christ, the joy just kept building until it became a part of who he was.

And I figured out where it came from...it came from the Bible. He was in his Bible his whole life, and knew the scriptures beyond what most of us could ever hope.

But the Bible, God's Word, spoke to him, and it filled him with joy.

My father was a lifelong evangelist.

I know you all know this, but it is a huge part of his legacy.

It was the overwhelming purpose of his life to tell as many people as he possibly could about his Savior, Jesus Christ.

No stone unturned, no opportunity passed by, no group of listeners too small.

He wanted everyone he met to know, to be saved, and to be with him in heaven.

Everyone.

That would be me...and that would be you.

It was why he asked me to speak today...he knew I understood his passion, because he knew it was mine as well.

Last fall, he told me that the best part of being sick, especially having cancer, was that people would listen to you when you talked to them, and that he had encountered many opportunities to share the message of the gospel with people who may not have listened to him otherwise.

Now that is a true evangelist.

It was never about him, how many he could save. It was always about lifting high the name of Jesus Christ, who died for each and every one of us. It was his gratefulness and awe for this salvation gift coming out in his words and deeds.

And so it is today...I know Dad does not mind me saying nice things about him as long as I give the glory to Jesus Christ for everything Dad was and everything good that he did.

You see, my father identified himself with Jesus Christ. I think of that, and of him, whenever I read this Bible passage:

"But whatever was to my profit I now consider loss for the sake of Christ. What is more, I consider everything a loss compared to the surpassing greatness of knowing Christ Jesus my Lord, for whose sake I have lost all things. I consider them rubbish, that I may gain Christ and be found in him, not having a righteousness of my own that comes from the law, but that which is through faith in Christ - the righteousness that comes from God and is by faith. I want to know Christ and the power of his resurrection and the fellowship of sharing in his sufferings, becoming like him in his death, and so, somehow, to attain to the resurrection from the dead." Philippians 3:7-11

And just as nothing in my dad's life was more important than knowing Christ Jesus his Lord, so it should be for me...and for you.

It's what Dad wants you to think about today. Where does Jesus Christ fit into your life? Is He everything to you, or have you put him in a closed box, and have you shut Him out altogether? Dad knows that you cannot have joy or peace without knowing Jesus Christ personally, and that was not only his last wish, but his lifelong wish for each one of us here today.

My father knew his eternal destination. He knew he would spend eternity with his Savior and King, Jesus Christ. He knew it because Jesus promised it, and he knew he could trust in those promises.

So he is now where he knew he would be, and yet it is undoubtedly more wonderful than he ever could have imagined.

I cannot begin to imagine all the people he is seeing there who are there because of his witness, and oh my, there are going to be so many more. So many who were introduced to Jesus Christ by my father in his lifetime on this earth.

I would be one of those people.

I know Dad hopes that you will be, too.

That is what he wants you to know...you can see him again, you can be with him in heaven, and this life is only the short and difficult beginning.

His life from now on is everlasting joy and glory.

My father wants that for you, too.

Your heavenly Father wants that for you, as well.

So you see, my father's legacy is all about what God was able to do in his life...and my father would have never wanted it any other way.

On Friday, God gave me this incredible opportunity to minister to my dad. One of the last things I did was read him this scripture, which really seemed to speak to him:

"Keep me safe, O God, for in you I take refuge.

I said to the Lord, "You are my Lord; apart from you I have no good thing."

As for the saints who are in the land, they are the glorious ones in whom is all my delight.

The sorrows of those will increase who run after other gods.

I will not pour out their libations of blood or take their names on my lips.

Lord, you have assigned me my portion and my cup; you have made my lot secure.

The boundary lines have fallen for me in pleasant places; surely I have a delightful inheritance.

I will praise the Lord, who counsels me; even at night my heart instructs me.

I have set the Lord always before me.

Because he is at my right hand, I will not be shaken.

Therefore my heart is glad and my tongue rejoices; my body also will rest secure, because you will not abandon me to the grave, nor will you let your Holy One see decay.

You have made known to me the path of life; you will fill me with joy in your presence, with eternal pleasures at your right hand." Psalms 16

# Chapter 19

# JARED'S STORY

"Blessed is the man who does not walk in the counsel of the wicked or stand in the way of sinners or sit in the seat of mockers.
But his delight is in the law of the Lord, and on his law he meditates day and night.
He is like a tree planted by streams of water, which yield its fruit in season and whose leaf does not wither.
Whatever he does prospers."
Psalm 1:1-3

"Precious in the sight of the Lord is the death of his saints."
Psalm 116:15

"When calamity comes, the wicked are brought down, but even in death the righteous have a refuge."
Proverbs 14:32

"Then I heard a voice from heaven say, "Write: Blessed are the dead who die in the Lord from now on."

"Yes," says the Spirit, "they will rest from their labor, for their deeds will follow them."

Revelation 14:13

March 14, 2007 was a normal Wednesday for us. But it was not going to end that way.

I went to church choir practice that evening as I always did, arriving home shortly after 9:00, and I sat down in the love seat next to Jackie just like I always do. We sat and talked, and half-watched TV. It was almost time to call it a day.

The phone rang at 9:30, and Jackie went to get it. I heard her talking, and just the tone of her voice gave me a sense of terrible dread.

After she hung up she came back in the living room, and her face was ashen.

"That was Nicole. Jared has been shot, and it doesn't look good."

A thousand questions flooded my mind all at once, but before I could ask them she told me what she knew.

"It happened in the armory in Guam. We don't know if it was intentional or an accident, but he was shot in the head, and is in the hospital on life support."

For us there was only one thing to do. We prayed.

We pleaded with God to save him, not to take him from us at age 24. Neither of us has ever prayed so intensely or so desperately. But we also believe that God's will is perfect, and we also prayed that we would not falter if it was His will not to save this beloved son.

Shortly after that we got the call.

Jared had gone home to be with his Lord.


A whole book could be written about Jared Krutke's life, and probably should be. He was an amazing young man. He was an inspiration to nearly everyone who met him, and to all who got to know him. He set an example of selflessness unlike I have ever seen in anyone, much less in one so young.

I could not write that book. Not that I wouldn't like the story told, but to be brutally honest it is hard enough for me to write this chapter.

But I know that God wants me to do this so that the meaning in Jared's life and death will continue to unfold to the glory of

God, and I know He will help me write it. Some things need to be written so that the lessons we can learn from Jared live on.

When I first met Jared he was just a boy. He and his brother Joe lived with his dad on the other side of the state, but they came to visit their mom, Jackie, from time to time. She was a good friend, and we often did things together anyway, so when her boys were visiting my son Justin and I would often spend time with them.

Jared was, to put it mildly, an energetic boy, but in a very positive way. He put everything he had into everything he did. This was a trait that would never change in him, and one God used in remarkable ways.

After Jackie and I were married, every time the boys came our house was a bit of a zoo, but very fun. Jared was a big part of that, and he and Justin became pretty good pals. Both of them loved the outdoors, and had more than a few adventures together. We did a lot of fishing, which always seemed to involve someone falling in the river.

When Jared reached high school age, he was struggling in school, and he and Joe came to live with us so Jared could attend the local Christian high school.

It was during these years when he lived with us that Jared became like a son to me. It was also during this time he accepted Jesus Christ as his Savior, and as the Lord of his life. His life took on new meaning.

It was also the time of his life when he met and fell in love with Nicole. I really believe that the "met" and "fell in love" happened at the same time.

Jared was not much of a reader, which really is a hindrance when you're trying to get good grades in school. His grades were touch and go, and he quite honestly graduated from high school by the skin of his teeth.

He did, though, read his Bible, and he was quite fascinated by it. He involved himself in youth activities at church, and he experienced extraordinary spiritual growth. God put a number of spiritually influential people in his life to build up his faith for the tests that would lie ahead.

Jared developed a close personal relationship with his Lord. Jesus was his best friend.

It is hard to describe the joy that permeated his life. He was not perfect, of course, and as a stepfather he would certainly frustrate me at times, but the love he had for his family, his friends, his lady, and his Lord was an amazing thing to observe. I did then, and still do now, consider it a gift from God to be a personal witness to Jared's growth as a young man and a follower of Christ.

Shortly after graduating from high school, Jared entered the Navy. He was, as you might guess, very enthusiastic about this, and so, of course, threw himself into it with everything he had. In short, he loved it.

During the first few months of training he was only a couple of hours away from our home, so most weekends I would drive down and pick him up on Friday afternoon, and take him back on Sunday afternoon. Most of those drives were just the two of us, and we had time to talk about a lot more than everyday kinds of things. We got into deep discussions about many things, but most notably about our shared love for Jesus Christ, and our concern for those who didn't know Him.

We also talked a lot about how you remain faithful to Jesus when you are in situations where it is a lot easier to try to fit in. I was in the Army, and I knew Jared would find himself tempted to deny his Lord to avoid being different.

It would later turn out that these conversations were orchestrated by God to prepare Jared for what would lie ahead. I often cling to the memory of those moments when I was granted access to the heart of this young man who truly loved his Lord.

When Jared was assigned to a ship, and did his first 6-month assignment out to sea, he took a huge step in his walk of faith. I like to think of it as standing between the world, with all its temptations of pleasure, and Jesus, with His promise of eternal joy and life.

This was the time in his life when Jared stood at that place, and the time when he made his decision which way he was going to go.

I know this because he emailed me every day. It was hard being a Christian in this environment, and he was struggling with all the temptations. There was a lot of free time on the ship, and little to do. Much of what went on he knew was not what he should be doing.

I reminded him many times to remember what gave his life meaning. But I also suggested that as a disciple of Jesus Christ he should follow the example Jesus set, one of growing closer to God and of serving others.

Jared made his decision. He stepped toward the Savior. Not just one step, either. He went all the way to the throne.

He became an enthusiastic reader. He read his Bible and every Christian book his mom would send him. Every box Jackie sent had snacks and books, and he shared the snacks, and read and shared the books.

He looked for, and found, ways to help others. Sometimes it was just listening, sometimes it was teaching, sometimes it was helping out with something that was not his job, sometimes it was just nice clean fun.

About a year later Jared and Nicole were married. To many it seemed a little crazy, them being so young, but Jackie and I knew this marriage was in God's plan. She was the love of his life, and remained so until his last moment on earth.

A couple of years later their daughter Elizabeth was born. Until that day I thought I had seen all the joy Jared had, but I was wrong. He was absolutely radiant when he held that little girl.

Jared had been in the Navy five years when his unit was split up between Iraq and Guam. Most of his unit went to Iraq, but when he and a few others were assigned to Guam, we were quite relieved. It seemed so much safer there.

Jared and two other sailors were assigned to the armory in Guam. Each day a different one of the three was assigned to carry a handgun. On this day in March the young man with the gun had a meltdown. When the other sailor made a comment he didn't like he pulled the gun out of the holster and shot him.

When Jared came running at the sound of the shot, the sailor shot him too, first in the leg and then in the head. He then set the gun down and walked out of the armory, calmly announcing that he had killed someone.

Jared lived a very short time before going home to be with the Savior to whom he was so devoted.

After we got the news, it was too late at night to call anyone. We sat and held each other on the love seat all night, sharing the emptiness and pain. It is impossible for me to describe it.

We prayed to God for comfort, and we asked him to let us understand at least a little bit of why this happened.

In a way, it was good that we had that night. We had only each other and God. We could not understand why it happened, but we decided that we were going to trust Him. He responded with comfort that only God can give.

In the morning, we told Justin and our daughter Jasmine what had happened. This was by far the hardest thing I've ever had to do as a parent. And yet, I could tell them with the greatest of certainty that their brother was now in the place that Jesus Himself had prepared for those who love Him...forever joyful.

I could tell you a hundred stories of the incredible response from friends and family when the news got out. There were phone calls, visits, emails, meals delivered, and more hugs than I could count. Every single one of them helped keep us going, and helped us trust God.

But let me tell you just one.

My friend Stan had been battling cancer. He had been in the choir with me, but had not sung in quite a while because of his illness.

On Thursday, we had decided that it would be too hard to do our usual duties at church. I sang in the choir, we both taught 3rd grade Sunday School, and together we taught Children's Church. But we got so many calls and notes from our Sunday School kids that we decided to go ahead and teach. We needed to show them that we were trusting God in this tragedy, and we wanted to experience their compassion.

By Saturday I wanted to sing in the choir, too, although I knew this would be hard and very emotional. The choir is like another family, and though I knew my being there would make it hard for everyone, I wanted to sing praises to God like never before.

The prayer time our choir had before we went on stage that Sunday was very emotional and yet very meaningful. Shortly after we walked out there, the side door opened, and Stan came out, music in hand, walked over, stood next to me, and put his arm around me. Tears rolled down my cheeks.

I have never sung or worshipped quite the way I did that day.

After we left the stage, I sat down in the choir room, emotionally spent. Stan came and sat next to me.

"Stan, what are you doing here?" I asked him.

"There's no way I was not going to be here for you today," he answered, and the arm went around my shoulders again.

"You've got enough problems of your own," I said.

His answer is one I will always remember.

"I've got nothing."

Because of the investigation into the shooting, and the autopsy that was required, it was two weeks before the funeral could be held. It was an amazing service, a testimony to a young man who lived for God and for others. The theme of the message was Jared's stated life purpose of living with "no regrets".

In other words, he lived his life in service to his Lord, ready always to meet Him face to face.

It was also a testimony to the power of saving grace.

A website was created to share pictures and personal stories about Jared. I want to share in this chapter two of the stories that so perfectly describe the man that Jared was.

"I am HT1 William Schweikert. I do not know where to start to tell you how sorry I am for your loss. I enjoyed every minute that he and I spent together. There is one time I remember my son, who was 4 at the time, asked him to shave his head and dress up as Darth Maul from Stars Wars so my son could be Luke, and he did, and off they walked having light saber fights down the street."

This one is from Kendra Cook:

"I didn't really work with Jared in NMCB 74, but I did work around him. During the first two months of our deployment here to Guam Jared became like my big brother. I was closer to him than I am to almost everyone in my family. And he treated me like I was his little sister that he had to watch over. I have a ton of stories, but there is one thing that he did for me that I will never forget. I had surgery on my knee on March 1st. I was bedridden and I couldn't even go to get my own food. Jared brought me movies to watch during the day while they were all at work. He would also stop by and bring me food...3 times a day. He always made sure to stop by and see how I was doing no matter what else he may have had to do. He would sometimes bring the guys down after work, or just come by himself, to watch movies and hang out in the room so I wasn't alone. We would all have a blast together and things would get out of hand as they all started to rough-house...but then there would come Jared's voice warning everyone else that they had better not hit my knee or they would have to answer to him. He made sure I had everything I could possibly need to be comfortable in that current state. He even went as far as to bring down an airsoft gun and a full bottle of little balls for it. He set up paper targets and numerous amounts of empty soda cans for me to practice my aim. And then he helped me clean up every single last bb that was on the floor or where ever they may have ended up. Now...for those of you who don't know...that's almost 3,000 of them. I never once saw him frown. He ALWAYS wore a smile on his face. Especially when we would talk about how much we missed home and when he talked about getting to see his wife and little girl again. He told me tons of stories about Nicole and Elizabeth, and I shared stories with him. I never had a single bad second around Jared. He was a gift from above. I never had a brother...I have two sisters. He watched out for and protected me...just the same as a big brother would do for his little sister. I will never forget the things he had done for me. As I heard a pastor say: "I don't think that any of us have lost Jared. How could we "lose" someone when we know exactly where they are? I know Jared is in heaven, and we will all meet him again." My thoughts and prayers are with his wife, Nicole, and his daughter, Elizabeth. It is a tragedy what happened, but I hope they both know how much he truly loved and cared for them."

We have witnessed many examples of how the lives of people who knew Jared have changed because of his death. We have seen God glorified as we all looked back on Jared's life, which was a testimony to each of us who knew him.

In other words, God has answered our prayer to know at least some of the reasons He allowed this to happen.

I call them "doses of grace", and they give me comfort.

There was a lot of talk for while about the injustice of Jared's death, and the man who shot him.

We have never focused on that. We know this world, with Satan's influence, is full of injustice. We also know that God will, in the end, bring justice to all for all time. That is His work.

Our work is to proclaim that a man like Jared, who made his stand for Jesus Christ, who made a decision to make his life about his Lord, had a life that made sense and that had purpose and meaning.

The reason? Because Jared surrendered his life to his Lord, and lived ready, with no regrets, to go to be with Him.

God, in His wisdom and grace, has made it possible for us to understand at least a part of why even Jared's death makes sense.

And if Jared was joyful here, imagine how joyful he is *there*!

Jackie and I continue to share what we have learned about our great and wonderful God in this experience. Shortly after the one-year anniversary of Jared's death we shared our testimony and sang a hymn in church to testify to God's amazing grace in the face of terrible loss. I close the chapter with both:

"Just a few weeks ago marked the one-year anniversary of the sudden passing of Jared Krutke, our beloved son and brother, into eternal life. His life was a beacon of light to all who knew him, and his death an unjust and unspeakable tragedy. But in the dark hours late at night when Jackie and I first heard the news, God demonstrated to us in a very personal way that His comfort, His love, and His grace are quite real, and His promise to be faithful to those who love Him took on new meaning. In turning to God in the worst moments of our lives we found our closure. Not only would God take care of us, but He now had Jared safe and happy for eternity, and we know we will see him again. God ministered to us whenever the pain and sorrow became too much for us, because He knows us intimately. He did it in many ways, but most notably through the hugs, tears, cards, visits, acts of kindness, simple words, and prayers of many of you. But God did more than that...much more. He allowed us to see how He could use this tragedy to soften hearts and bring others into His Kingdom, and how our trusting Him in this time of loss could bring glory to His Holy Name. This song is not in tribute to Jared, though we are so proud of the life he lived and the man he was...committed to God, family, friends, and country. It is in tribute and praise to the God who sent His Son to die that we might have forgiveness of sins, and victory over death and its cruelty. We are witnesses of the faithfulness and grace of God in the darkest hour. Whatever you may be facing, today or in the future, no matter how big or small, we want you to know God knows what you are going through, He is always right there for you, and He has everything under control for all eternity."

### Be Still, My Soul

Be still, my soul! The Lord is on thy side; Bear patiently the cross of grief or pain;
Leave to thy God to order and provide; In every change He faithful will remain.
Be still, my soul! Thy best, thy heavenly Friend thro' thorny ways leads to a joyful end.

Be still, my soul! Thy God doth undertake to guide the future as He has the past.
Thy hope, thy confidence let nothing shake; all now mysterious shall be bright at last.
Be still, my soul! The waves and winds still know His voice who ruled them while He dwelt below.

Be still, my soul! The hour is hastening on when we shall be forever with the Lord.

When disappointment, grief, and fear are gone, sorrow forgot, love's purest joys restored.

Be still, my soul! When change and tears are past, all safe and blessed, we shall meet at last.

# Part III

# LIFE AFTER LIFE AND DEATH

# Chapter 20

# CHOICES

"Brothers, we do not want you to be ignorant about those who fall asleep, or to grieve like the rest of men, who have no hope. We believe that Jesus died and rose again and so we believe that God will bring with Jesus those who have fallen asleep in Him. According to the Lord's own word, we tell you that we who are still alive, who are left till the coming of the Lord, will certainly not precede those who have fallen asleep. For the Lord himself will come down from heaven, with a loud command, with the voice of the archangel and with the trumpet call of God, and the dead in Christ will rise first. After that, we who are still alive and are left will be caught up together with them in the clouds to meet the Lord in the air. And so we will be with the Lord forever.
Therefore encourage each other with these words."
I Thessalonians 4:13-18

"Then I saw a great white throne and him who was seated on it. Earth and sky fled from his presence, and there was no place for them. And I saw the dead, great and small, standing before the throne, and books were opened. Another book was opened, which is the book of life. The dead were judged according to what they had done as recorded in the books. The sea gave up the dead that were in it, and death and Hades gave up the dead that were in them, and each person was judged according to what he had done. Then death and Hades were thrown into the lake of fire. The lake of fire is the second death. If anyone's name was not found written in the book of life, he was thrown into the lake of fire."

Revelation 20:11-15

"Then I saw a new heaven and a new earth, for the first heaven and the first earth had passed away, and there was no longer any sea. I saw the Holy City, the new Jerusalem, coming down out of heaven from God, prepared as a bride beautifully dressed for her husband. And I heard a loud voice from the throne saying, "Now the dwelling of God is with men, and he will live with them. They will be his people, and God himself will be with them and be their God. He will wipe every tear from their eyes. There will be no more death or mourning or crying or pain, for the old order of things has passed away." He who was seated on the throne said, "I am making everything new!" Then he said, "Write this down, for these words are trustworthy and true." He said to me: "It is done. I am the Alpha and the Omega, the Beginning and the End. To him who is thirsty I will give to drink without cost from the spring of the water of life. He who overcomes will inherit all of this, and I will be his God and he will be my son. But the cowardly, the unbelieving, the vile, the murderers, the sexually immoral, those who practice magic arts, the idolaters and all liars - their place will be in the fiery lake of burning sulfur. This is the second death."

Revelation 21:1-7

Five months after Jared died I said goodbye to my friend Bill. Bill was 51 years old when he died, and his death came out of nowhere. He didn't seem to have any physical problems of any consequence and seemed to have many years of life left.

But Bill died of a heart attack sitting in his favorite chair in the basement sometime in the night, surrounded by all of his favorite electronic and technological gadgets, and his wife Sue found him the next morning.

While I will admit that I dealt with Bill's sudden passing much better because of what I had already been through that year, there was something different about this one.

I do not know what choice Bill made.

Numerous times throughout the years I knew Bill we had this discussion about what happens when you die. I would tell him what I believe, which is based on what the Bible teaches. Our choice in life to acknowledge Jesus as Lord and Savior and to follow Him results in the reward of being with Jesus forever in a glorious heaven. Our choice in life to deny Jesus results in the punishment of eternal torment in hell.

Bill's viewpoint was that when you die, that's it. No more consciousness, no more life, no more awareness of anything.

When I asked him the basis of this belief, he would always tell me that since there is no proof of mine, since no one has ever come back after dying to confirm my belief, there is no reason to believe there is any life after death.

I would then remind him that there is One who rose from the dead, who defeated death so that we might have eternal life.

That one perfect One is Jesus Christ.

But Bill remained, at best, skeptical.

However, something that was said at Jared's funeral, which Bill attended, seemed to have made him rethink his position on this. There were words which God had someone say at that funeral that reached into Bill's heart and mind, and I know he had at least begun to wonder whether he might be wrong about that.

I never got the opportunity to explore this with him, so I don't know where he went with it. I don't know whether Bill ever did business with God, if he ever acknowledged Jesus Christ as Lord, and so I don't know where he is.

And though I hope and pray that he did, and I like to believe that God was extra gracious and gave him the opportunity to do so right at the end of his life, not knowing is difficult.

I am buoyed by the knowledge that even if Bill made his confession in the very last moments of his life that God would honor his choice to spend eternal life in heaven with Him.

At Bill's funeral, I said, among other things, these words:

"Bill was the hardest man to argue with I have ever known. He had the softest, kindest way of disagreeing with you. He certainly had to have a very forgiving heart, because I'm certain most of us here must have annoyed him at some point, but you would never know it. I'm not really sure why he was that way, but it was such a great quality about him. God is like that, too. He has taken each of us, with all of our stubbornness and self-ishness, tenderly in His arms and offered us forgiveness for every single sinful act we've ever committed. All we have to do is acknowledge His free gift to us, the sacrifice He made for our forgiveness, His Son Jesus Christ. I truly believe that if Bill could speak to us today from beyond the grave, he would want us all to know that."

There are many amazing things about God, but to me one of the most amazing is that not only is this brief life not all there is, but that He lets us each choose where we wish to spend the eternity that follows this life.

And our choices are as different as two things can possibly be.

We can choose to accept his free gift, eternal life in a place He has prepared for those who love Him, and be in His very presence forever.

Or we can choose to reject Him and be in pain and torment forever.

What is so hard to comprehend is that most people will make the second choice.

It seems ridiculously foolish to choose to do whatever you want for 60 or 70 or 80 years, and suffer punishment for it *forever*.

It especially seems foolish when you think about the alternative. If we commit our life to Jesus Christ for whatever is left of it, no matter how much or how little, we will be rewarded with a life of pure joy and peace, free of pain or sorrow or tears or heartache, *forever*.

Grasping this idea of "forever" is an important part of deciding what choice you will make. We have a hard time getting our minds around how long forever is because it actually can't be done. Since there is no end to forever, we can't measure it or compare it to something else. It is simply so long a period of time that we will never see it end.

But when you sit and think about the truth that when you die, there will only be those two options, the ultimate in wonderful and the ultimate in terrible, and that both last so long that we cannot imagine or understand, the magnitude of your decision begins to take shape.

There is another very important point to be made about this choice that every human being makes.

The choice must be made during this lifetime.

If the choice could be made *after* you die, I'm sure *everyone*, seeing the two choices firsthand, would choose to spend eternity with God in heaven. They would choose everlasting joy over being in a lake of fire.

But the choice must be made in this life, and since we don't know how much time we have left, putting off choosing God's joyful home is very risky and dangerous.

So *when* you decide to accept Jesus Christ as Savior, and as Lord of your life, is pretty important, as well.

The sooner you make that decision and that commitment, the better. Not only to insure your place in heaven, but to guarantee that nothing that happens in this life can change where you are going when this life is over. There is nothing that anyone can do to you in this world and in this life that you cannot handle because your commitment to the choice God wishes for you puts you very close to Him, and you can trust all things to Him from that point on.

And though God will allow you to make that decision at *any* point in time in this lifetime, even in the last moments before your death, and will still reward you for your choice of His Son, making it sooner offers assurance and comfort to those left behind when your life ends.

They will know where you have gone, and Who you are with. That thought will give them great comfort and peace.

Making your choice sooner will also give you more time to tell other people about your decision, and offer you more opportunity to express your desire to see them in heaven when you get there.

Some people will tell you that they have not made a choice, but I'm here to tell you that everyone has. If you have not acknowledged God's Son as Lord, you have chosen a life after death in which the pain will never end, one in which you will wish you could die, but you cannot.

The question is, what choice have *you* made?

I might be able to tell, or at least guess, by the way you live. I might know if you told me and if I could see that it was true.

But there are only two who know what choice you have made.

That would be you and God.

If you have chosen to surrender your life to the One who made a way for you to be saved, your life now will make sense. The assurance of your eternal future gives you a hope and a peace that cannot be found any other way.

If you have chosen to spend eternity with Him, your death will also make sense. It is nothing but a doorway to eternal joy and happiness. When you die, those left behind will have the comfort of knowing that you are in the loving arms of Jesus.

I know you know what I want you to choose. It is the same thing God wants you to choose. I know He wants you to choose to be with Him because He sent His Son to die for you so that you could have that choice.

And so you must choose.

The best time to do that would be today.
Then tomorrow life would *really* begin.
And it would last forever.

# Chapter 21

# JUDGMENT

"All who sin apart from the law will also perish apart from the law, and all who sin under the law will be judged by the law. For it is not those who hear the law who are righteous in God's sight, but it is those who obey the law who will be declared righteous. This will take place on the day when God will judge men's secrets through Jesus Christ, as my gospel declares."

Romans 2:12-13, 16

"Enoch, the seventh from Adam, prophesied about these men: "See, the Lord is coming with thousands upon thousands of his holy ones to judge everyone, and to convict all the ungodly of all the ungodly acts they have done in the ungodly way, and of all the harsh words ungodly sinners have spoken against him."

Jude 14-15

"If we live, we live to the Lord; and if we die, we die to the Lord. So, whether we live or die, we belong to the Lord. For this very reason, Christ died and returned to life so that he might be the Lord of both the dead and the living.

You, then, why do you judge your brother? Or why do you look down on your brother?

For we will all stand before God's judgment seat. It is written: "As surely as I live, says the Lord, every knee will bow before me; every tongue will confess to God." So then, each of us will give an account of himself to God."

Romans 14:8-12

"I don't believe that a loving God will judge people guilty and send them to hell."

A man I know, we'll call him Jim, made this statement. We were having what could be called a theological discussion, although truth be known we were really talking about matters of such importance that you might say it was a matter of life and death.

I have had this conversation with many people before, and yet I am always puzzled and frightened when I hear it. So I asked Jim what I always ask anyone who says something like this.

"On what do you base this belief?"

Jim's answer was classic.

"Well, God is a loving God, right? And He wants us all to be with Him in heaven, right? And He understands that we are human, and that we make mistakes, but He knows that we are doing the best we can, right? So I believe He will look at all the good things we did, and overlook the bad things because our heart was in the right place."

"So, do you believe there is *anyone* who is going to hell?" I asked him.

"Well, I suppose the really awful people might," he replied.

"Do you believe God is holy?" I asked.

"Of course."

"And since God is holy, and without sin, do you believe He will not tolerate sin?"

"Yes, I believe that."

"So on the day of judgment, if a sinful, unforgiven man stands before the throne, will God judge him guilty or innocent?"

"Well, guilty, I suppose."

"So will that guilty man go to heaven?"

"Well, I guess it depends on how bad the sins are."

"But if God will not tolerate any sin, wouldn't all sins be bad?"

"Well, yes, but I think some are worse than others."

"What about your sins? Are they bad sins or "not so bad" sins?"

"I would say my sins are not so bad."

"So what you are telling me is that you are willing to take the chance that when you stand before the throne of God on Judgment Day that God, who is holy and will not tolerate any sin, will overlook yours because they're not that bad?"

"I guess I'll just have to," Jim replied.

My thought when he said that was, "No wonder people are so afraid of death."

Jim is wrong about that last statement. God has made it very clear that we can *know* our eternal destination after we die. The reason we can know is because we make that choice in this life about His Son, Jesus Christ.

God's own words tell us that if we accept His Son as Savior, and as Lord of our life, if we trust Him alone to save us from eternal hell, we will stand before God on the Day of Judgment pure and spotless, free of sin, because our sins will have been totally forgiven by the sacrifice that Jesus made for us on the cross.

Our judgment will be one of what level of reward we receive by virtue of the deeds we have done in this life. The extent to which we have served Him will determine not *whether* we are rewarded, but *how much*.

God's words also tell us that if we never acknowledge and accept His Son, we will die in our sins and stand before Him on Judgment Day condemned by the sins we committed to spend eternity in hell, a place of torment and pain.

Does this mean God is not a loving God? By no means!

In fact, it's just the opposite. Because God knew that we could never manage to live a life without sinning, He made a way for us to have that sin washed away and forgiven so that we could spend eternity with Him.

The only way it could be done was for His own Son, Jesus Christ, to come to this earth, live a perfect, sinless life, and be killed by sinful men as the sacrifice for us. He then rose from the dead in victory over the ultimate death, which is eternal separation from God.

Does a God who would do that for you seem like a loving God?

He sure does to me. What could be harder than to give up your own child and allow him to be murdered before your eyes to save other people?

How much does He love you?

Enough to do that so that you could be with Him forever.

We can stand before Him with no fear and no sin to condemn us.

That's what a loving God does for the ones He created.

There are some misconceptions and falsehoods about Judgment Day that are quite popular. They are based on delusions and wishful thinking, and have evolved as a result of mankind's selfish desire to live for self instead of for the Creator.

One of them is just what Jim verbalized, that God will look at a person's life and somehow measure the good against the bad, and determine that there is enough good there to outweigh the bad. There is no evidence of this anywhere in the words and promises that God has given us.

It is a popular belief because it is a way of justifying sin. If we compare ourselves to other people, especially those who are clearly worse than us, we look pretty good.

The problem is that on the Judgment Day we will not be compared to other people. We will be compared to God, and judged by His standards.

It is probably a good idea to note here that God's standards are based on perfection, something we cannot achieve without the help of the One who came to save us by dying on the cross for our forgiveness.

It is also important to look into the Bible to see what God calls sin. Lying, disrespect to parents, unrighteous anger, lack of forgiveness for others, sexual immorality, pride, wanting something that belongs to someone else, and even evil thoughts are all examples of sin that God will not tolerate, and thus that we need to be forgiven.

And while we might view these as "not so bad" sins that God will overlook at the Judgment, He says otherwise. In fact, He lumps these kinds of sins together with ones like murder and theft...to Him they are all sins, and they are all punished the same way.

So while it might feel good to think that being a "good person" in general is going to be enough to get by on the Day of Judgment, God says otherwise. And He is the final and ultimate and only Authority from beginning to end.

A second falsehood that is popular is that God will take into account special circumstances when He judges you. If you had parents who were cruel to you, He will overlook sins you committed as a result. If you were always poor, He will overlook your lack of generosity. If you meant to do a lot more nice things for other people, but were too busy, He will understand and let it go.

Again, there is no basis for this belief. It is based on the assumption that we can be forgiven by standards of forgiveness that we ourselves set.

And when it comes to ourselves we are *very* forgiving.

With others...not so much.

Many years ago a business mentor of mine gave me a tremendous piece of advice. He told me this simple thing:

"Never burn a bridge with anyone. You will almost always end up regretting it."

I have tried very hard to follow that. There are times when we'd really like to give someone a piece of our mind, and if we do we have destroyed the connection, the bridge if you will, with that person for good.

But when we do that, we have judged that person as unworthy of us, and judged ourselves as superior to them, forever without need of them. And how often does it happen that we find ourselves needing them for something, and we have made it impossible to go to them for their help.

People often "burn the bridge" with God, choosing to live in a way that they know does not please Him, because of their sinful nature and selfish desires. They like to think that they will make it right with Him when they stand before His throne, apologize and He will forgive them, sending them to heaven because of their penitence and humility before His throne.

But the thing is, they will not be standing.

They will be kneeling.

The Bible says that "every knee will bow" and "every tongue confess that Jesus Christ is Lord" (Philippians 2:10-11).

In other words, everyone will be a believer on the Day of Judgment. Everyone will be penitent and humble.

To be penitent and humble before God for the first time on that day will be too late.

There will be no special exemptions or special circumstances, and we will not be our own judge.

One other commonly believed falsehood is that despite our guilt when judged, we will be granted eternity in heaven anyway.

The thinking here is that God will give us the benefit of the doubt, so to speak, and because we are so cute or nice or lovable, in the end He will be unable to pull the trigger and send us to hell.

God is loving and God is just. Those two attributes of God go perfectly together. He will not only judge perfectly based on the standards He has made very clear to us, and which have never changed, but He will see that His perfect justice is carried out.

Even in our world if you are found guilty of something in a court of law, there is a penalty. There is a sentence and it will be carried out. There is no such thing as being found guilty and then set free without any consequence.

People who believe in this delusion believe in a god who is weak, and who does not keep his word. I don't know who that god is, but it is not the true and living God. He will have the ultimate and perfect justice.

Those who have defied Him will no longer do so on the Day of Judgment, but it will be too late for them to change the verdict or the sentence.

I, for one, am glad about that. I want to be in a heaven filled with people who loved and feared God in their life, not just when the reality hit after their death.

As a financial advisor, I have prepared over a thousand retirement financial plans in my career. Not a single one of them recommends buying lottery tickets throughout your working life, hoping to win sometime before retirement age, as a way of funding retirement income needs.

Trying to work your way into heaven, trying to do enough good things to squeak by and hoping that God will overlook the sins, is like buying lottery tickets to fund your retirement, except that with the lottery tickets, despite terrible odds, there is actually a chance it could succeed.

With God, there is only one way, but there are no odds. It is guaranteed.

Jesus said, "I am the way and the truth and the life. No one comes to the Father except through me."

There will be a Judgment Day. God, who is the Authority over each of us and everything in the heavens and the earth, has said it, and thus it will be.

But we don't have to be afraid of the Judgment, you know. God has told us how we can kneel before Him in reverence, then stand before Him with absolutely no sin to keep us from heaven.

I, for one, can hardly wait for that moment.

And I really hope you are there with me.

# Chapter 22

# DESTINATION

"The Son of Man will send out his angels, and they will weed out of his kingdom everything that causes sin and all who do evil. They will throw them into the fiery furnace, where there will be weeping and gnashing of teeth. Then the righteous will shine like the sun in the kingdom of their Father. He who has ears, let him hear."

Matthew 13:41-43

"Therefore do not lose heart. Though outwardly we are wasting away, yet inwardly we are being renewed day by day. For our light and momentary troubles are achieving for us an eternal glory that far outweighs them all.
So we fix our eyes not on what is seen, but on what is unseen. For what is seen is temporary, but what is unseen is eternal."

II Corinthians 4:16-18

"The Spirit and the bride say, "Come!" And let him who hears say, "Come!"
Whoever is thirsty, let him come; and whoever wishes, let him take the free gift of the water of life."

Revelation 22:17

I took one of my informal and very unscientific surveys for this chapter.

I asked this question: "What do you think heaven is like?"

All of the answers were different, and yet they were all the same.

Lest you think I've lost my mind, let me explain what I mean by that.

They were all different, because everyone imagined something that they really liked.

Here are some samples:

"All my favorite foods will be available all the time, and I'll never get full or gain weight."

"There will be lots of dogs."

"There will be lots of cats."

"There will be non-stop music, and it will be the most beautiful music ever heard."

"Everyone will be smiling."

"My arthritis will be gone."

"There will be golf, and I will be good at it."

"I will see my parents and grandparents again."

"I will be a good singer."

Those, by the way, were all from adults. The best one, though, came from one of my third grade Sunday School boys:

"Jesus will be there."

Interesting, huh?

They were all the same, though, because the questions caused everyone to think of the most wonderful place they could possibly imagine, a place where there was nothing but joy.

I followed up this question with another question.

I asked, "Do you think you are going there?"

I only got two answers: "I hope so" and "I know I am."

I also asked them all this question: "What do you think hell is like?"

About a third of the people to whom I asked this question said something like this:

"I don't believe there is a hell."

My follow-up question to them was "So is everyone going to heaven, or is there some other alternative place?"

There were really no answers to that question. They either said "I don't know" or mumbled something that didn't really make sense.

The other two-thirds gave me answers to my question "What do you think hell is like?" that were pretty much the same. Here are some samples:

"Hot."

"Awful."

"Scary."

"Painful."

I found that no one really wanted to elaborate on their answers. In fact, they didn't seem that thrilled that I asked them the question.

Then came my follow-up question: "Do you think you are going there?"

Again, I only got two answers: "I hope not" and "No."

So, you may ask, what conclusions did I draw from my survey?

My conclusions were:

Most people have correctly grasped the nature of heaven and hell.

Most people live in delusion about the reality of who and how many will go to each place.

Many people have no idea where they are going.

What is really fascinating and amazing is that God has made certain to tell us enough about our two potential destinations so that we have no doubt or misunderstanding, and He has even allowed us to choose the one we want.

Now I'll be the first to admit I would like to know more about heaven, but I understand that my human mind is not capable of understanding or even imagining how beautiful and wonderful it will be. I do know enough, though, to know I would very much like to go there.

So I have chosen to do just that.

How? By trusting His Son, Jesus Christ, for my salvation. By making my life on this earth not about me, but about Him.

When I first made this decision, I thought it would mean my life would be nothing but sacrifice and hardship to gain the greater glory, eternity in heaven. But what I found out instead is that a life lived for Jesus is a life of joy no matter what comes my way.

My life has purpose and meaning. It makes sense. Best of all, I know where I am going when this life is over. And I know I'm going to like it because Jesus will be there, and I *love* Jesus because of who He is and what He did for me.

The Bible doesn't give us a lot of details about heaven, but there are some things it does tell us. We are told it is a glorious place, and that the life we live there will be free of pain or sorrow or death. There will be lots of singing, and I assume that means we'll all be doing it very well. There will be lots of worship, because God will be there, and Jesus will be there.

If you like worship, you will love heaven. Can you imagine what worship will be like with the One you are worshipping sitting right in front of you?

Wow!

Heaven will be beautiful. This for sure we cannot begin to imagine. I often look out at my back yard, which is large and surrounded by tremendous tall trees, and I marvel at the beauty of God's creation. But it is clear when you read about heaven that it is way beyond what we have seen, and even beyond what we can imagine.

God has saved His best creation work for heaven, and He has given us something to look forward to. The anticipation of what is coming next makes death a whole lot easier to deal with.

My best friend Dana's dad died last week. He was a great man of God. He loved Jesus, and he made sure everyone he met knew that. When he found out he was terminal, Dana asked him if he was afraid.

"No," he said. "I'm looking forward to it. I've never died before, so I don't know what it will be like, but I'm excited to see what comes next."

Now there was a man who trusted God's promises.

And for good reason.

To me, the best thing about heaven is revealed in John 14:1-3. Here is what it says there:

"Do not let your hearts be troubled. Trust in God, trust also in me. In my Father's house are many rooms; if it were not so, I would have told you. I am going there to prepare a place for you. And if I go and prepare a place for you, I will come back and take you to be with me that you also may be where I am."

The best thing about heaven is that it was designed by Jesus just for those who love Jesus.

The Creator of the universe, the One who knows me best, has prepared this place for me, this place that He knows I will really love.

At that thought I am way beyond awe.

Oh yes, and did you notice that Jesus will be there with us? My Sunday School boy had it right.

And while we love talking about and thinking about heaven, we are just the opposite when it comes to hell, as my little survey would indicate. In fact, there are many people who refuse to believe there is a hell.

However, like many unpleasant things, it is a reality whether we acknowledge it or not. Denying its existence does not make it go away. It is very real.

And it is far more than unpleasant. It is your worst nightmare multiplied a trillion times, except that you never get to wake up.

There is actually more written in the Bible about hell than about heaven. Descriptions of it involve torment, pain, suffering, darkness, a lake of fire, weeping, gnashing of teeth, and eternal punishment.

It is a place reserved for those who deny the Creator, God Almighty, and His Son, Jesus Christ, the Savior of the world.

Is this just? Of course it is.

What makes it just is that we do not have to go there, and God will not send us there without our permission. We give permission by denying Him in this life.

Is God trying to scare us? In a way, yes.

He wants us to completely recognize Him as the ultimate Judge, and to understand the consequences of denying Him. He wants us to know the power He has, and to face the reality of both of our possible destinations after this life is over.

He wants there to be no doubt in our mind that hell is not a place we want to spend eternity, and that accepting His Son will keep us from going there.

But beyond that, accepting His Son will give us peace and joy and meaning in this life as well, not to mention a glorious reward for eternity in heaven.

God does not want us to live for Him *solely* because of our fear of hell, but He does want us to think about it and accept the reality of it. He wants it to be a part of our thinking process in making a decision in this life regarding His Son.

Most people would not choose to go to hell. No one in my survey did. But there are some who claim they would prefer to go there.

My dad and I used to discuss this on occasion because we did not agree on it. We had both had people tell us they were going to hell, and who said they were just fine with that.

When people have said this to me, I have always felt just heartsick for them, and tried to explain what hell is like. I always felt they just weren't well enough informed, that if they understood hell better they would change their mind.

My dad believed that, although they did have misconceptions about hell, and that they would wish they weren't there once they were, they would not like heaven. He always said that if you don't love Jesus, you won't love heaven.

He may have been right, and yet we both agreed on this:

If you get to know Jesus, you will love Him. And once you love Him, you will absolutely love heaven.

I know quite a few people who are in heaven now, and I am so happy for them. Though I miss them here, I know someday I will be with them again, sharing joy every moment of every day.

What a cool thought that is!

So it comes down to these two possible destinations.

191

God says you can pick the one you want, but you have to do it now. The moment you die, the decision is made and can no longer be changed.

Therein lies the key. If you deny Him in this life, He will deny you after this life ends. If you glorify Him in this life, He will glorify you in the next life.

And the next life is forever.

Although nearly everyone *would* choose heaven, many have not made that choice because it involves putting aside our selfish desires in this life. They have, at least so far, chosen to try to find happiness in this life. They have, of course, had no success, and their life is not making much sense. All their joys are brief and temporary.

Only in Jesus Christ can you choose heaven. Putting Him first will give you peace and joy and a life that makes sense now. It will also give you joy beyond your imagination in the place He has prepared for you in the future.

So make your choice, but make it now...today.

I hope you choose heaven. I'd love to see you there.

Oh, and did I mention the best part?

Jesus will be there.

# Chapter 23

# DURATION

"Do not be deceived: God cannot be mocked. A man reaps what he sows.
The one who sows to please his sinful nature, from that nature will reap destruction; the one who sows to please the Spirit, from the Spirit will reap eternal life."

Galatians 6:7-8


"God is just: He will pay back trouble to those who trouble you and give relief to you who are troubled, and to us as well. This will happen when the Lord Jesus is revealed from heaven in blazing fire with his powerful angels.
He will punish those who do not know God and do not obey the gospel of our Lord Jesus. They will be punished with everlasting destruction and shut out from the presence of the Lord and from the majesty of his power on the day he comes to be glorified in his holy people and to be marveled at among all those who have believed."

II Thessalonians 1:6-10a

"And this is the testimony: God has given us eternal life, and this life is in his Son. He who has the Son has life; he who does not have the Son of God does not have life."

I John 5:11-12

"Now this is eternal life: that they may know you, the only true God, and Jesus Christ, whom you have sent."

John 17:3

I f you want to hear some interesting thoughts, ask someone this question:

"How long is forever?"

You can just see the wheels turning as you watch the person you asked grapple with how it might be explained.

The best answer I ever heard came from a deeply insightful 9-year-old boy in my Sunday School class.

"Longer than we can ever imagine," he said.

I believe he hit the nail on the head.

The dictionary defines forever as a "limitless time". When I read that, I decided that it did not help me get a handle on it. I think the 9-year-old made more sense.

We can try to imagine what forever is like, but we really can't, because it will mean there would be no reason to even keep track of time, and keeping track of time is kind of a big deal with us.

Think about it...birthdays are pretty important to a lot of people.

And even though we can't quite get our mind around how long forever is, we really need to think about it, because we are all going to be somewhere forever.

We have already determined what those two possible destinations are, and that we get to choose the one we want.

But we really need to think about the undeniable fact that whatever we choose will be forever, and that makes our choice of destinations the most important decision we will ever make in this life.

So what is it you would like to be doing forever?

Some things in this life are so good that we *think* we'd like to be doing them forever. There are, for example, some foods we eat that are so incredibly tasty that we think we'd like to eat them every day for the rest of our life.

We have a garden, and though it is a good sized garden, we plant it every year with nothing but green beans. We all really like green beans, which is good because when the plants mature and we get a harvest, we eat a *lot* of green beans. We eat them pretty much every day for weeks and weeks, and even end up giving a lot of them to friends in a good green bean year.

When we eat that first batch of green beans, they taste *so* good that we all feel like we'd like to eat green beans every day for the rest of our life. Of course, living in Wisconsin, that is not possible, which is probably a good thing because I feel fairly certain that at some point we would not relish eating green beans with quite the same degree of enthusiasm.

We have relationship moments in our life that we wish to relive day after day forever, too. Someone does something incredibly and amazingly wonderful for you, something you will never forget, and you find yourself wishing to have that moment over and over again.

Or how about the first time you realize you really love someone? Wouldn't you like to have that day every day?

There are some days about which we might even say "I wish this day could go on forever."

The really cool part is that if you choose heaven, it can.

And then some!

Just as we cannot understand the real meaning of eternity, we cannot grasp the incredible wonders we will experience in heaven, amazing and joyful moments that will go on and on and on and on....

Because God is our Creator, and knows things about us we ourselves have yet to learn, He will be able to give us an eternity of experiences more wonderful than any we've ever had or even been able to imagine. Endless joy, ceaseless elation, and love beyond expression will be our every moment.

After all, God is love, and we will be with Him.

Wow!

I think it's safe to say that the reward that God will give to those who love Him, and who have been devoted to Him during this short life, will be the kind of reward that only a God with unlimited power and love could dream up.

If you choose heaven, you are going to like it, and you are going to like it every moment forever.

Lest this leaves you, like me, feeling quite undeserving of such a place and such a life for such a long time, keep in mind that Jesus paid your way because He loves you so much He wants you there.

Once you grab hold of this truth, not just in your mind but in your heart, you are going to start loving Him back.

And that love is going to grow, and as it grows you are going to get closer and closer to Him, and you are going to treasure the thought of an eternity that you get to be with Him.

While He was on this earth Jesus liked to talk about the rewards ahead for those who love and obey Him. Though He understood that we cannot grasp all of it, He knows how much we will love the place and future He has prepared for us. He knows we will treasure every moment for eternity infinitely more than the greatest moment we ever had on this earth and in this life.

That, my friends, is some kind of love He has for us.

But we also have those moments and days in this life that we hope to never relive, that cannot end soon enough, don't we?

We have those times when something goes so horribly wrong. We experience pain, physical or emotional, so intense that we never forget what it was like. We just want it to be over, and yet the effect of it and the memory of it lingers.

Though we don't want to linger on those moments, it is important to think about them because they come to us for a reason.

Our eternity could be just like that.

We could, after this life is over, have an endless experience of that kind of pain.

While it seems obvious that no one would ever choose that for their life, many people will choose that for their eternity.

They will do so by choosing to reject Jesus Christ.

Many people are deluded about this, choosing to believe that it couldn't possibly be that bad, or that God will in the end not be able to send them to hell, even if by their life on this earth they have clearly chosen to go there.

Lest you have any doubt, think about the term the Bible uses to describe the eternity of those who live for themselves in this life and who reject God and His Son.

The term is "everlasting destruction."

This is a description so frightening that it is hard to conceive in the mind. If you've ever had a time in your life where you felt like your life was destroyed, then imagine every moment forever being like that.

When we think of destruction, we think of it ending. When something is destroyed, it is totaled, done, ended. But this everlasting destruction the Bible describes sounds to me like a nightmare where every moment another possible way of escape closes off.

And this nightmare goes on forever.

I know you're thinking I'm simply trying to scare you, but I'm not. I am really just portraying the reality of the eternal future of those who reject their Creator, and who choose to decline the gift of eternal life He has offered.

It is important to fear God. He has the power to carry out perfect justice, and He will do exactly that one day.

But we do not have to be *afraid* of God, because He does love us, and He did an incredible thing to prove it, and to make a way that we might be with Him forever.

His justice is perfect, and He will not compromise it one bit. You will either get the eternity you deserve, or you will get the eternity Jesus has secured for you.

In this life we have good days and bad days. When this life is over, our eternity will either be nothing but the best days ever or nothing but the worst days ever.

Not only do we get to choose our eternity, but we get to make the decision and *know* our eternal destination *now*.

The way we live our life now tells us what our choice is. We either live our life to serve and please ourselves, in which case our eternal future is everlasting destruction, or we live our life to serve and please God, in which case our eternal future is never-ending joy.

And while we may be able to fool people around us about what our choice is, we cannot fool God. There are lots of people who seem "religious", or who do a lot of nice things for other people, whose hearts do not belong to God. They do what they do for recognition, or with the belief that they will earn an eternal reward with their deeds.

Perhaps you're one of those people.

But only a heart that is submitted to Jesus Christ will do.

And God knows what's in the heart of every one of us.

What is so wonderful is that when the heart belongs to Jesus Christ, the life we live here, this temporary short life, suddenly has purpose and meaning, and the forgettable or bad days have far less consequence or effect on us. Our choice to spend eternity with Him takes away all our anxiety and uncertainty about not only what happens to us in this life, but what happens to us after we die.

My favorite devotion book is called "My Utmost for His Highest". It is a collection of teachings by Oswald Chambers. He himself did not write this book, but his wife put it together after his death. She had recorded things he said, and I must say they are amazing and profound.

I am on my fourth time around on this book, because in the one page I read each day there are truths about God that are stated in ways that challenge me and hold me accountable. I need and appreciate that.

One of the things Chambers said that stuck with me was this: "there is no heaven that has a little corner of hell in it."

It challenges me to look at my life and realize that I am either all in for Jesus Christ or I am not at all.

There isn't going to be a heaven not quite as nice for the people who "tried" to live a good and moral life.

There isn't going to be a hell not quite as bad for the people who weren't as bad as other people.

There will only be two eternities, and the standard to determine which we have earned will be God's standard.

We either love and trust His Son or we don't.

We get to choose...eternal life with Jesus or eternal destruction without Him.

Forever is a long time.

Longer than we can ever imagine.

# EPILOGUE

Every day you read things and are told things that are not true.

Some of the time it is intentional.

Some of the time it is not.

The problem is in trying to sort out the true from the untrue, and the intentional from the unintentional.

Where we often go wrong in trying to do this is in believing that others would never tell us something that is untrue, intentionally or unintentionally. We believe this because *we* would never do so, and because we want to believe that people are basically good.

But we have all been disillusioned to learn that we have been told something that is simply not true, and it has happened to us many, many times.

Perhaps at this stage of your life you are not sure what is true and what is not. Perhaps you're even wondering how much of what is written in this book is true.

I want you to know that I am okay with that skepticism. I believe it is healthy.

But here is the important thing: you must have a source of absolute truth to be able to measure the degree of truth in what you read and hear.

This is so critical because in this life there must be something or someone you can believe in that is unchanging. You must have a foundation of truth in order to have hope and joy and peace.

If you wonder whether there is a God who created you, or if you suspect there is, or even if you know there is, then you have to realize that this is the road you must go down to find that absolute truth.

And that truth is found in the very Words of the God who created you.

That truth is in the Bible.

Reading it will change you.

Studying it will challenge you.

Living it will encourage you.

To make sense of your life, it begins with understanding the significance to *you* of the very first words in it:

"In the beginning God created the heavens and the earth."

Once you grasp the enormity of this truth, that there is a Being with enough power to create everything you see around you, you begin to realize that nothing that exists is an accident. Everything has a purpose.

Including you.

As you read on, you get the specifics of what God created and when, including His creation of man and woman, and realize that your very existence, your life, is by His intention. You are not here without a purpose.

God is the authority over all things. This is true whether you acknowledge it or not. But once you *do* acknowledge it, once you stand outside and look to the heavens and declare to Him your belief in Him, you have declared your understanding that your life has meaning.

God meant for you to be here.

Many intelligent people have tried to come up with some kind of an explanation other than that God created everything. You and I may not have a PhD, but if we look at these alternative theories, we instinctively know they are not true.

Why? Because God gave us an understanding in our inner being that He exists, and that He is indeed the ultimate and final authority over all things.

In the Bible you will not read very far before you get to the part where the first man and woman sinned against God. From that point on all human beings were born with a sinful nature, and separated from God by that sin.

So, you see, people are not basically good. People are basically self-serving.

As you read on, you encounter people just like you and me, people who intend to do good, who try to live good lives, who try to be faithful to God. Sometimes they are successful, sometimes they are not. Just like us they have their moments when they think only of themselves and their desires, and they, even if only briefly, forget about God.

In other words, they sin.

You also encounter people who have every intention of doing evil, people who try to improve their position at the expense of others, whose lives are all about their pleasure all the time. Deceit of others is to them a perfectly acceptable way to get what they want.

Though we may not be people like this, we know people like this. Many people who have risen to positions of power in this world are people like this. We hear their deceitful words all the time. They are not hard to spot. They do or say whatever will get them what they want.

As you read in the Bible about these people, you begin to realize that there are two types of people.

There are those who believe in God and who want to serve Him, but who often fail Him.

And there are those who put their personal desires ahead of all else, whether they believe in God or not.

As you read on it becomes obvious that this pattern of human behavior will go on until God ends it or changes it. Mankind needs saving.

And then you come to the Savior.

You come to the part where God sent His Son, Jesus Christ, down from heaven to live on earth, to represent Him perfectly, and to break the pattern. Jesus lived a perfect life on earth so that He might take on *our* sin and become the sacrifice that granted us permanent forgiveness.

You are amazed when you realize that there were people who hung out with Jesus and who witnessed His Words and His miracles that still didn't believe in Him. Some of them believed after He died on the cross and rose from the dead, but many still didn't.

And so it still is today. There are people who have been introduced to Him by someone, who have perhaps even witnessed a miracle that can only be from Him, who still deny Him. They are all about themselves, in hot pursuit of some kind of satisfaction and happiness in this life.

As you read about what God did to save the ones He created, and as the realization sets in that He sat there in heaven with all the power and watched as mankind tortured and murdered His Son, you begin to understand the importance God has placed on you and how incredibly much He loves you.

Reading on, you understand that to access forgiveness of *your* sins, and to secure a place in heaven with God forever, requires action on your part.

It is simple, really. It does not involve studying theology, or going to church, or involving yourself in some righteous act. It does not require you to try to earn a ticket to heaven by being a good person or doing good things.

You only have to acknowledge what Jesus did to save you, and to allow His incredible act of love to truly sink in. When it does, you will kneel before God, asking for His forgiveness for all your selfishness and sin, and you will find the focus of your life change from *you* to *Him*.

The search for meaning and purpose in your life will have come to an end. You will know that your life is all about making known who God is, and what He has done. You will spend the rest of your life thanking Him with your words and your actions because you have trusted Him for your salvation and with your life.

And every day will have meaning, because the Creator has granted it.

Perhaps you *will* study theology. Certainly you will want to go to church and find others who have also committed their lives to

Him. You will absolutely look for every conceivable way to serve Him and to point others, especially those you love, to Him.

You will want to share the joy you have found and the hope that you are now sure of.

As you read to the end of the Bible, you find out how it all turns out in the end. You will discover that there are those two eternal destinations.

And you will know which one you have chosen.

There are so many wonderful things about God, but one of the best is that He has revealed to us everything we need to know. He has put it all in a book, the Bible, which mankind in his sin has tried to get rid of, deny, or re-word throughout all history without success.

It is the foundation we need. It is that source of truth which we can use to measure all that we read and hear.

That includes this book that you have just read. What I have said in this book should be measured against the truth in God's Word.

Some of the lies that you read or hear are intentional. They are deceitful statements made by someone who wants you to believe them for their own selfish purposes.

Some of the lies that you read or hear are unintentional. They are statements made in ignorance or delusion. They may even be easy to believe because we think they will make our lives easier, or because we would be able to justify something we are doing that is nagging our conscience.

But truth is not a changing, evolving thing. It is truth yesterday, today, and forever, and it is undeniable.

Only God, the Creator of all things, the perfect and holy One, can declare truth. And He has given us the truth about every-thing we need to know to live meaningful lives, and to never live in fear of the end of this life. Living in His truth means under-standing that death is a doorway to a beautiful future.

God asked me to write this book to point the way to Him. He wants you to know how to find Him, because knowing Him is the only way you will ever make sense of life and death.

I know this because He has taught it to me.

He taught it to me because I wanted to know.

Through the lessons I have learned so that I could write this book, even the very hard ones, and throughout the writing of this book, He has been faithful.

I have given you what He asked me to give you.

Now it is up to you.

Trust Him.

CPSIA information can be obtained at www.ICGtesting.com
Printed in the USA
LVOW130122210613

339563LV00003B/8/P